MANIFEST THE LIFE YOU LOVE

UNLOCK THE POWER

OF YOUR STORY

HQ
An imprint of HarperCollinsPublishers Ltd
1 London Bridge Street
London SE1 9GF

www.harpercollins.co.uk

HarperCollinsPublishers
Macken House
39/40 Mayor Street Upper
Dublin 1
D01 C9W8
Ireland

10 9 8 7 6 5 4 3 2 1

First published in Great Britain by
HQ, an imprint of HarperCollinsPublishers Ltd 2025

ISBN 978-0-00-876914-7

Publishing Director: Louise McKeever
Book Design: Steve Wells
Editor: Rachael Kilduff
Senior Production Controller: Halema Begum

Printed and bound in Bosnia and Herzegovina by GPS.

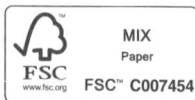

MIX
Paper
FSC
www.fsc.org   FSC™ C007454

For more information visit: www.harpercollins.co.uk/green

MANIFEST THE LIFE YOU LOVE

UNLOCK THE POWER

OF YOUR STORY

Carolyn Boyes

HQ

An imprint of HarperCollinsPublishers Ltd.

CONTENTS

INTRODUCTION

'Magic's just science that we don't understand yet.'

Arthur C. Clarke

Welcome to *Manifest the Life You Love*.

Let me start by asking you a few questions.

※ How do you feel about your life? Happy, fulfilled? Have you created the life you once imagined for yourself?

※ What would you wish for if you could have anything? A new job, more friends, a new home? A great love? Your heart's desire?

Where you are today is the accumulation of everything that has happened to you so far in your life. Each one of us has taken a series of paths – either by accident or by choice – to end up where we are. Your current life has been determined by every thought and feeling you have had, every action you've taken and all the people and circumstances you have attracted along the way as a result.

Think about it. Everything that exists began with a thought, a picture in someone's mind. In every garden, seeds had to be planted before the flowers could bloom. The amazing technology we all have in the phones in our pockets came about as the result of imagination, focus and intention. Every time a new medicine is discovered and developed it is the end result of many different wishes – the child who wished to become a scientist, the student who dreamed of running a company, the adult who had a vision of making a difference to people's lives.

Most of our lives appear, falsely, to be determined by luck and chance. In actual fact, I have met many successful people who credit amazing changes in their lives to the power of manifesting: multi-millionaires, businesspeople, philanthropists, as well as people who are simply content all round. Despite appearances, we are all equally powerful. Wherever you are in your life, at any second, minute, day, month or year, you have the option to continue your current path or pause and ask yourself: what do I want now in my life? Once you can imagine it, you can manifest it.

Even before I knew anything about manifesting, I was aware that if you really focused on a specific dream that you wanted to attract into your future, somehow things would work out and you would be very likely to get it. However, it was only as I experimented in my own life that I began to see that something more was happening than just my working hard towards a goal. Somehow, when I truly determined what I wanted, it was as if everything fell into place and I just seemed to attract good luck. I discovered that the power of manifesting and the law of attraction were at work in my life.

I've now been writing about manifesting for more than twenty years. In that time, I've learned how to overcome barriers to success and make consistent manifesting easy. But beneath every technique, one truth stands out: the stories you tell yourself *really* matter. They shape your entire reality – not just how you see the world, but what you believe is possible within it. That's what this book is about. It invites you to see your life as a story – with you as the main character. And it shows you how to rewrite that story with clarity, purpose and creativity. Drawing on the tools of great storytelling – character arcs, turning points, inner conflict, resolution – you'll learn to uncover the beliefs that are holding you back and reshape the narrative that defines your future. When you work with your story at this level, you don't just shift your mindset – you change your trajectory.

My goal is to help you become the author of your own life. By the end of this book, you'll be writing a new version of your future – one that's not only aligned with what you want, but grounded in a deeper sense of what's truly possible. After all, sometimes reality just needs a good edit.

'The universe is full of magical things patiently waiting for our senses to become sharper.'
Eden Phillpotts, *A Shadow Passes*

HOW TO READ THIS BOOK

This book offers a clear blueprint for manifesting the life you love. I've broken the process down into seven simple steps – each with examples and exercises to help you get clear about what you want, understand how to manifest most effectively, and overcome any obstacles that have held you back in the past. The order of the steps is important, but it can be helpful to read through them first and then return to the exercises if you prefer to have the full picture before you begin.

The ideal way to read this book is from front to back, treating it like going on a journey, or reading a novel. Spend as much time as you like on each chapter and have fun with the exercises. You can come back to them again and again. Instead of sticking this book on a shelf after you've read it through once, please use it as a place to jot down thoughts. Underline what makes an impression on you, use colour and highlighter pens, and fill in every exercise that takes your fancy. There are no rights and wrongs in the answers you give. There is only a journey of self-discovery.

As you read through this book, you will find out what stories you tell yourself and how they relate to how successful you are in your manifesting. You will discover precisely how can you edit your life and build a new world for yourself. And when you're ready, you'll find your 12-month journal waiting for you at the end – a space to ground those changes in daily life.

Why not make your coming year the very best one of your life?

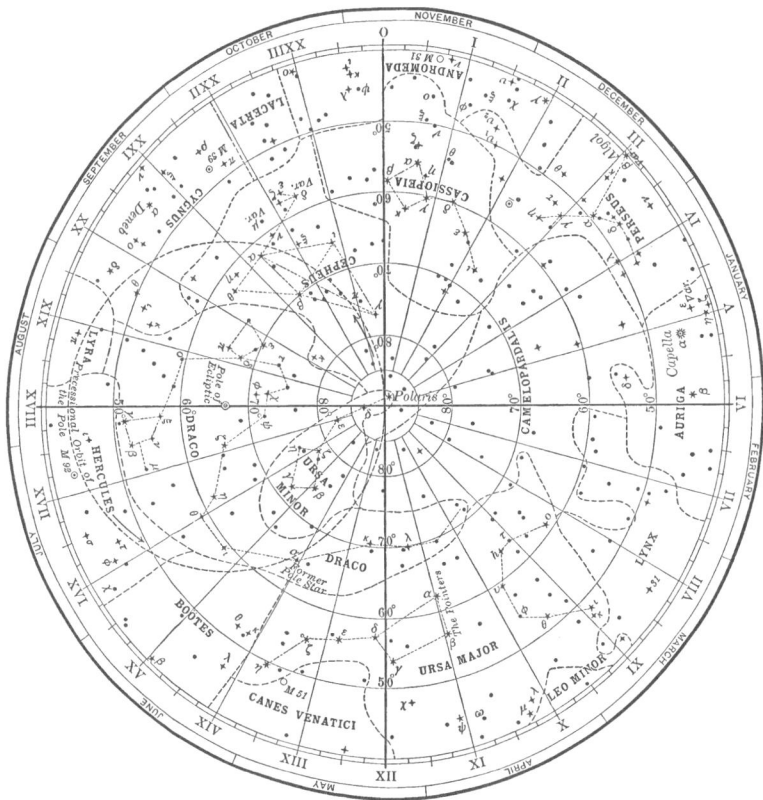

MANIFESTING
BASICS

'We all can dance when we find music that we love.'
Giles Andreae and Guy Parker-Rees
Giraffes Can't Dance

M anifesting is the practice of focusing your thoughts on what you want, in order to turn your dreams into reality. This concept goes by many names: cosmic ordering, visioning, the law of attraction. The underlying idea is that by visualising and then focusing on the outcomes you want, and by acting as if your goal is already happening, you start to bring those outcomes into your life.

At the heart of manifesting are three core principles:
1. Pay *attention* to what you want by making a wish.
2. *Intend* that this wish will come true – focus your energy on it.
3. *Expect* it to happen, and stay open to however the universe delivers it.

Manifesting can apply to many areas of your life. For example, you might want a new career: visualise yourself with the new job title, thriving in your new role or passing the final interview. Perhaps you want to manifest financial abundance: imagine receiving a particular

sum of money, or enjoying what it allows you to do. You might want to attract a healthy relationship: see yourself with your future partner, experiencing joyous moments. Feel yourself worthy of unconditional love.

If you imagine a confident version of yourself, moving through life and having new experiences that bring growth and adventure, you will begin to manifest it.

MANIFESTING VS. SETTING GOALS

When you're young, you don't think twice about making wishes. Growing up brings an end to this. Instead of wishing for things, adults set goals.

If you've set goals before, you may have done so using methods like SMART: deciding what you want to achieve with an exact timeframe and a measure of success before setting out a series of actionable steps that will take you towards that goal. When you begin, you know exactly what you must do to get what you want. Setting goals requires logic, effort and willpower. Goals can be hard work.

Manifesting, in contrast, should feel easy. When manifesting, you also begin by imagining something you want. However, unlike with setting a goal, you don't need to know exactly how you are going to make your dreams come true; your picture of what you want is the important thing. When you manifest, you use focused thoughts, feelings and belief mindset changes to attract what you want – and when it appears, it is often as if by luck or synchronicity. You don't need to know *how* – you just need to know what, and to trust the process.

THE ROLE OF THE UNIVERSE

When you manifest something, the universe becomes your co-creator. By crafting your wishes effectively, you are in collaboration with the fundamental life force in the universe. You can surrender the 'how' in favour of intention and an expectation that you will be rewarded.

The universe is more than the world of the senses. It exists on levels beyond the comprehension of your ability to see, hear and touch. The material world and the invisible world are both made up of vibrating energy, sometimes called electro-magnetic energy. What surrounds us may look solid and hard, but this is an illusion. Everything is made up of energy. Take radio waves, for example – we can't see them, and until relatively recently in human history they would have seemed like magic. But now, of course, we accept that many things exist beyond our ordinary senses.

You are a powerful vehicle through which the life force of the universe flows. This life force connects you

to everything that exists in the world: every atom and molecule and every other human being. The *Emerald Tablet*, an ancient Hermetic text on alchemy, describes this energy as a force that 'vanquishes every subtle thing and penetrates every solid thing'.

At a quantum level, science posits that everything that comes into existence manifests as waves of energy, leading to deep levels of interconnectedness. Our thoughts and intentions, also being energetic in nature, interact and influence the fundamental fabric of the universe. When you craft your wish, you send a ripple through the universe which eventually brings your wish into reality.

THE ALIGNED SELF

Think of yourself as composed of three parts:

- ※ Your conscious, which thinks it's in charge.
- ※ Your subconscious, which stores your memories and sense of identity.
- ※ Your higher self, which is connected to the invisible universe.

From childhood you begin to build a story about yourself and everything around you in the world. These generalisations, personal interpretations and theories about life are accepted and stored in the subconscious. These decide your past, present and future reality. It's like having your own personal library stored inside you, with new books added throughout your lifetime. Some will be helpful, but others will have titles like, *You Can't Have What You Want and This Is Why*, *Why You're Useless at Love*, or *You'll Never Be Rich and Don't Deserve to Be Anyway*.

If your conscious and subconscious are not aligned in their belief that something is possible, then the subconscious wins out. To make sure you manifest all your goals successfully, your subconscious must fully buy into your conscious desires. This is the Law of

Attraction: your thoughts attract precisely what you expect to attract into your life.

When you make a wish, you don't just manifest something material – you gain spiritually. If you don't change each time your manifest, you won't be able to manifest anything very meaningful because the Law of Attraction will just keep magnetising the same old stuff.

THE POWER OF INTENTION

We each have our own paths through life. Some of us are drawn to the spiritual journey and, if this is you, manifesting may encourage you to explore the deeper aspects of your life. My manifesting journey has revealed the interconnectedness of everyone. It has proved to me the perfection of karma. We must each act with good intentions and not, for example, wish to gain power over others. Likewise, if we judge or hate others rather than love them, it comes back to us threefold.

When I studied the shamanic tradition of *Huna* in Hawaii more than twenty years ago, I learned about how important focus is to creating magic. What you focus on is what you get. The stories we tell become significant – as you will see in the next part of the book.

THE MASTER
STORY
PATTERN

Many of our most popular myths, legends and fairy tales tell the same story. The main characters in these stories all embark on a similar kind of adventure: they leave the familiar behind, face obstacles, and ultimately return transformed. These stories teach us that we can reap amazing rewards once we learn to overcome our self-imposed limitations.

If you read enough of these stories, you'll start to see a pattern. There are usually two common themes:

1. An adventure in the real world: The main character starts off living a normal life, but they then have a choice presented to them: they are called to go on an adventure. They may resist at first, but eventually they leave the security of what they know to make the journey. The path is filled with challenges, but the main character wins out: they get the treasure or reward, slay a monster or achieve a personal goal.

2. A personal transformation: These journeys are transformative. They are journeys of self-growth, discovery and development. The main character gains as much in terms of personal growth as they do in terms of material success.

This pattern is known as 'The Hero's Journey'. This term was coined by American writer Joseph Campbell in his influential book *The Hero with a Thousand Faces*. For our purposes, we'll call it 'the master story pattern.' You'll find this pattern in stories everywhere: from *Alice's Adventures in Wonderland* to *The Lord of the Rings*, and in fairy stories such as *Hansel and Gretel* and *Cinderella*. It has been used by generations of novelists and filmmakers to create compelling plots, because this tale of someone who goes on an adventure is true to all of us. The main character begins the story as an ordinary person with no idea of what power lies within them. Surely and steadily, they move forward in search of treasure. They complete the journey with their goals accomplished and an understanding of their own abilities.

The main character is like us. They want a sense of purpose. They want love. They want to overcome fear. They want to experience something outside the ordinary. They want to find their true self. They want o achieve their heart's desire.

THE MASTER STORY PATTERN

In *The Hero with a Thousand Faces*, Joseph Campbell breaks the Hero's Journey into 12 steps. I have distilled the master story pattern into just seven steps, making it easier to apply to your manifesting journey. These steps will help you plot your journey from wishes to reward just as a writer plots a story. They are:

1. Our main character begins life in their ordinary world – until they are called to adventure. Often they refuse the call at first because they aren't ready to leave their normal life behind.

2. They accept the call to adventure and go off to find the treasure or reward. Often they meet a mentor – such as a wizard or fairy godmother – who helps them to accept the call.

3. They leave behind the comfort of what they know and go down a new path, crossing the threshold into a new life.

4. They meet allies – people who will help them along the path, even when they are being tested by enemies.

5. They reach the turning point of their journey. They are beginning to develop and change. Their very identity and sense of who they are is evolving.

6. They approach their 'innermost cave'. This is the greatest ordeal that the main character will encounter on this journey. They are challenged to see if they are ready to achieve what they want and, as a result, they shed their old identity.

7. They find what they are seeking – reward and resurrection. They gain self-knowledge and a material prize.

After reaching the reward, the main character returns to the same place they began their journey. The difference is that they have taken a transformative journey and so can never see the world in the same way they used to see it.

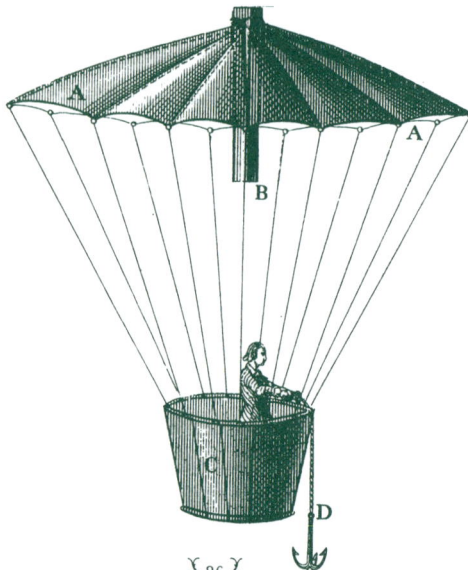

STEP-BY-STEP BREAKDOWN: *CINDERELLA*

Let's break down a well-known fairy tale – *Cinderella* – using the master story pattern.

1. Cinderella's ordinary world is a life of servitude. Her call to adventure comes when a royal ball is announced, but she's forced to refuse – forbidden to go by her stepmother.

2. A mentor appears, the Fairy Godmother, who uses magic to prepare Cinderella for the ball, helping her accept the call and believe a different life is possible.

3. She crosses the threshold from her kitchen to the palace, stepping into a new world of possibility.

4. At the ball, she faces tests and enemies – her stepmother and stepsisters – but she also has allies in her godmother and animal friends. Her bond with the Prince begins to grow.

5. As midnight nears, she reaches a turning point. She flees before revealing her identity, now caught between two worlds – servant and something more.

6. The Prince's search with the glass slipper marks her greatest ordeal. When she tries it on, her true self is revealed, and she leaves her old identity behind.

7. Her reward is love and a new life – but also transformation. She has grown stronger, stood up to her stepmother, and brings kindness and justice to her kingdom.

HOW WE CAN USE THESE STEPS ON OUR MANIFESTING JOURNEY

I've given each of these seven steps a name so you can easily see exactly where you are on your path. They are:

1. THE ORDINARY WORLD

2. THE WISH

3. BEGIN YOUR NEW LIFE

4. HELP IS HERE

5. YOU ARE TESTED

6. THE APPROACH

7. THE REWARD

When you manifest, you dream and you imagine a different version of your life. There is a gap between when the seeds are planted and when your desires manifest, and in that gap you change. When you collect your reward, you are different. How different, exactly, is determined by the magnitude of the wish.

You are both the author of and the main character in this story. You get to decide how the story unfolds. You have full creative control – and I'm hoping you're going to write a captivating read with a happy ending. Once you've made your first wish and started the journey, this book becomes a guide. It will help you understand exactly what stage of the adventure you have reached and how to get to the next stage, no matter what the obstacle.

And remember, you're also the editor. You can revise your wishes at any point. Your reality is in your hands.

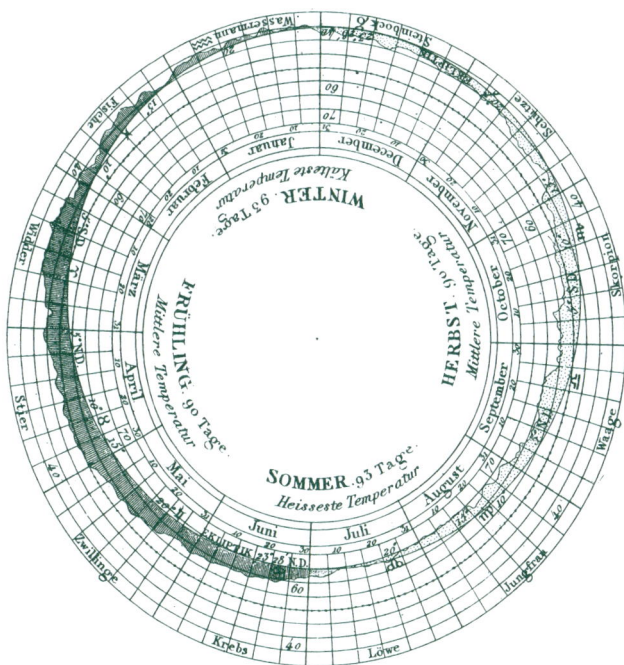

STORY: MY CALL TO ADVENTURE

I made a wish when I was nine years old which changed my life. It came true 10 years later.

With his green uniform and matching cap, the man was staring at me as if I was the strangest thing he had ever seen in his life. It would have been inconceivable to him that a small group of Western teenagers would be here in this dusty city in the north of China, after all these years closed off to outsiders. Behind him, a group of women with pigtails sticking out from their green caps had their eyes fixed on me in wonder and curiosity. In fact, a crowd of about 300 people had gathered along the dusty pavement outside the Number One Store to watch my friends and me try out the new bicycles we had just bought. There were hardly any cars, just hundreds of bikes lined up along the road.

I was a naive nineteen-year-old, and I was a long way from the English countryside where I grew up, but I was finally here. Somehow the mad dream I had had 10 years ago had come true; I had arrived in China to study Chinese. It was the early 1980s, and the country had only recently opened up to foreign investment and tourism. I had received a letter two weeks before I was due to leave with the name of the city where I would be studying. I hunted for it on my map, but the names were all spelled in an old-fashioned way, so I wasn't sure where I was heading. Instead, because I trusted everything would work out, I got on the plane with one large bag stuffed full of clothes which were somehow meant to see me through the next year. I met up with the small group of other students, and we set off on a journey from Hong Kong through mainland China by steam train. China is a very different place now, but at that time there were very few foreigners who had travelled there. Nothing could have prepared us for the amazing experiences and difficulties we would face. By the end of the year, I had become a very different person.

TEN YEARS EARLIER

I was an imaginative child who loved stories. Even at age nine I half-believed in magic, and my mind was full of happy endings. There was a pile of *National Geographic* magazines I sometimes looked at. They featured photographs of exotic places: seas, deserts and mountains, old buildings and archaeological discoveries. My grandparents and great-grandparents had travelled the world. Both grandfathers had worked in intelligence. My grandmother had lived in Russia before the revolution of the twentieth century. My father's father had been in China at the turn of the same century. We lived in a small village in England and we didn't have much money, but our cupboards still contained many of the objects inherited from my grandparents' travels – including one of Winston Churchill's cigars. But the objects that interested me the most had Chinese writing on them. I wondered what they meant.

Living in a small village, we didn't meet a huge variety of people. My mother had an old friend who lived in a large house on the Isle of Mull off the west coast of Scotland. A few months after my ninth birthday, we took a train to Scotland and crossed the sea by ferry. The trip didn't start off well. I was excited to swim in the loch that morning. Unfortunately, we were not the only guests in the cold water – a herd of sheep and several Highland cattle had got there first. When I got out of the water, my whole body was covered in ticks, which my mother and our hostess picked off me with a hairbrush. I was so embarrassed. That same evening, I had to join a formal dinner with plenty of local guests, all of whom seemed to be laughing at what had happened to me.

There was one man in his thirties who was sitting apart from the others. He caught my attention straight away because he had a parrot which was perched on his shoulder. What's more, he spoke Chinese! It was like something out of a story. I wondered if I could ever do anything as exotic in my life as learning to speak Chinese. If I did, it would take me far away from home; but surely if my ancestors could do it, so could I?

And so I made a wish. I wished that one day I would go to China – wherever that was. I wished I could speak Chinese. I visualised my goal clearly, and it started to become a reality. Though I didn't realise it at the time, I was about to step over a threshold in search of my treasure. A decade later, I found myself in China.

Even at this point, after my first wish had come true, I had no idea what would come next. My wish took me in all sorts of unexpected directions: from the trading floors of Asia, to meeting spiritual teachers, politicians and businesspeople, to becoming a writer. I now understand how a wish can change your life forever in amazing ways you can't anticipate. You will never be the same person that you were at the beginning of your story.

STEP ONE:

THE
ORDINARY
WORLD

'Well, maybe
it started that
way. As a dream,
but doesn't
everything?'

Roald Dahl
James and the Giant Peach

A story is a way of creating meaning and structure out of chaos. We all have lots of stories about ourselves. Some are happy, some are sad, some are dramatic, some are dull. I can narrate my life as one continuous story from the moment I was born, or I can break it up into meaningful chunks, each with its own beginning and ending. I can identify common patterns which occur in each segment. I can see turning points where I altered my perspective or took a decision which took me down an unexpected path. The most significant stories in my life, however, are the ones I deliberately dreamed into existence.

You are now ready to begin authoring the story you want to exist in your future. Most stories begin at the point just before a wish is made, in the ordinary world. Right now, you too are in the ordinary world, going about your normal life. You are Harry Potter before he receives the letter from Hogwarts, or Bilbo Baggins before Gandalf arrives, or the children before they find the back of the wardrobe that leads them to Narnia. Nothing changes until you make your wish. What the author understands – that the main character doesn't – is that the main character is full of untapped power and potential.

You have both an ordinary 'internal world' and an ordinary 'external world'. Your *internal world* is how you see yourself: your identity, values and beliefs about the world and yourself, whether empowering or limiting. Your *external world* is the world you have manifested around you. Your reality is composed of your unintentional and intentional manifests in all areas of your life: your relationships, material success, career and well-being.

The main characters of the most captivating stories possess both a compelling external desire – the treasure they seek in the material world – and a compelling internal desire – what they want to change about themselves. By identifying your deepest desires and turning them into wishes, you will leave behind the ordinary world and the old stories about yourself and craft an amazing life.

ABOUT YOUR ORDINARY WORLD

Before you make your first wish, let's take a look at your world right now: the ordinary world.

※ The ordinary world can be a comfortable place to be for a while because it's familiar and feels safe. It can also be an uncomfortable place that you stay in because of a fear of the unknown.

※ The ordinary world is where you end up when you don't pay attention to what you really want in life and when you don't intentionally manifest or wish for anything.

※ The ordinary world is where you live when you are afraid of failing or following your own path, when you don't love yourself, and when you don't have a good sense of who you are or what you can become. It's a world where you don't recognise your potential and power.

※ The ordinary world is the world you find yourself in when you aren't receptive to opportunities and don't expect to get what you want. It's full of feelings of 'I have to', 'I should' and 'I ought to'.

In the ordinary world, change can look intimidating. Our expectations of the future are shaped by our past experiences which keep us stuck in our habits, whether they are comfortable or uncomfortable.

IT'S NEARLY TIME TO CHOOSE...

You are almost ready. Your future is waiting to be written by you. Ahead of you lies an infinite number of doors, each opening onto a unique path and a different life. You can choose any door you want. If you choose a door and walk through it, you're going to meet new friends, find your power, and ultimately gain a reward. This reward can be anything you can imagine.

If you make big wishes, you will transform. Even if you stay in the same job, living in the same house and married to the same person, you *will* change. You will be more powerful than you were before, and more knowledgeable about yourself. But between making your wish and reaping the reward, time must pass, because we are in the world of time, space and matter. You have to know that you can stick to the path.

THE FOOL'S THRESHOLD

Have you ever seen the picture of The Fool in a deck of tarot cards? He stands at the edge of a cliff, ready to step into the unknown. This character symbolises

THE FOOL.

optimism and a positive belief that everything will turn out all right. The Fool is sometimes naïve, but he is also ready to trust and take a brave step. Like The Fool, you too hold the key to your own evolution. Just a moment away is all the freedom and fulfilment you could ever desire. Will you choose to take the leap?

'The privilege of a lifetime is to become who you truly are.'

Carl Jung

ABOUT YOUR NEW WORLD

As soon as you make a wish, you step into your new world.

- ❈ In your new world, you are going to discover your potential and become the extraordinary individual you've always been inside.
- ❈ In your new world, you can manifest whatever you want and whatever you are receptive to.
- ❈ In your new world, if you keep going you'll find what you are looking for.
- ❈ In your new world, the universe will bring you unexpected luck.

START IMAGINING

Children are great at writing at stories. It's a skill I need you to find again. Do you remember being nine years old? What did you dream of having? Who did you dream of becoming?

Every child has a wish they hope will come true. To an adult, a child's wishes seem impossible, but children are more in tune with their dreams. They ask, 'why can't I?' and 'what if I?' To a child, the world seems huge and full of possibilities. An adult seems to have magical powers because they can do things a child can't. Children's stories teach the lesson that you can make a wish and have a life full of magic and happy endings. It's unsurprising therefore that children spend about two-thirds of their time in their imagination.

As we grow up, however, our magical thinking changes. Schools stop giving us books with happy endings and make us learn facts and logic. We begin to believe that there are impossibilities as well as possibilities. We no longer believe in magic. In Western society where logic rules, adults tend to reinforce that logic is the right way to think. I read once that adults are 96 per cent less creative than they were when they were children. Other research has shown that those of us living in the West are all becoming less creative and imaginative. Of course, you need to have logical thinking to survive as an adult, but this should not be at the expense of your ability to imagine.

If you can't imagine, you can't create new ideas; without new ideas, you can't manifest an alternative to your current reality. It's vital to unlearn anything that gets in the way of your wishes coming true. It's time to get your imagination working again. If you've lost that innocent belief you used to have that anything is possible, start bringing that belief back. You have a blank page in front of you to begin creating your story. Dream it, and start writing.

'Faith means believing the unbelievable. Hope means hoping when everything seems hopeless.'

Gilbert K. Chesterton

STEP ONE
RESOURCES:

UNLOCK
YOUR
POTENTIAL

For each step of your journey, I've included resources to help you formulate your thoughts and get focused. Start by taking a deep dive into your current beliefs and the world you have created. Then, to help you to get your imagination going, write down your thoughts about possible futures.

EXERCISE: MY LIFE SO FAR

In this first exercise, I invite you to look at your stories. How would you describe your life so far? You don't need to think about this too much. It's better to write it instinctively, in one go, describing your life in the way you normally describe it to yourself and others.

Ask yourself: What's my life been like up until now? What do I tell myself about my life? What do I tell others about my life? Write out your story.

As you write out your story, notice any 'hot' words – words that trigger strong emotions, whether positive or negative. These are indicators of areas you should focus on keeping, or deleting, in your next life.

When you have written out the story of your life so far, pause and reflect on it. Who are you in this story? What's the current plot? Where is this story likely to lead you?

EXERCISE: MY WORLDS

This second exercise is very simple. Use the four questions below to review your current situation from every angle. It's useful to write down the answers so that you can come back to them from time to time and check what has changed in your thinking.

1. Think of a normal day.

2. Think of how you would like the day to be if *things in your life* were different.

3. Think of how the day would be if you were different.

4. Think of what your life would be like if it was filled with lots of different days like this.

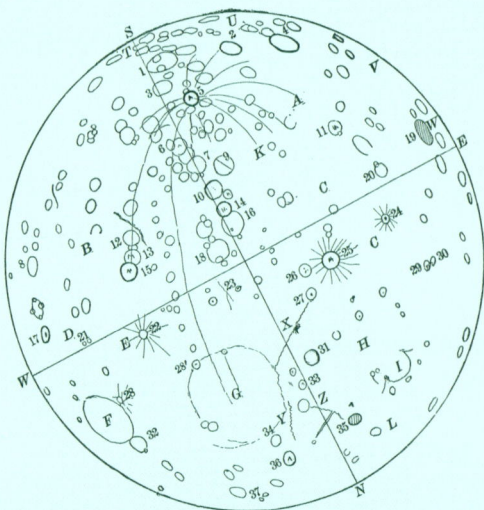

EXERCISE: ALL THE LIVES
I COULD EVER LIVE

In Matt Haig's bestselling book *The Midnight Library*, the main character explores all the different lives she could have lived through a library. Each book represents an alternate life she could be living. Imagine a bookshelf with three to five books in front of you. Give each book the title of a life you could have led. For example:

❀ Book One: *The CEO of a Tech Company*

❀ Book Two: *The Professional Artist*

❀ Book Three: *The Business Tycoon With a Global Charity*

❀ Book Four: *The Traveller Who Lived in Five Countries*

❀ Book Five: *The Woman Who Never Took No For an Answer*

Choose your own meaningful titles. Using a clean sheet of paper for each book, describe the story of the life you could have led. You can even draw an image for the book cover.

Look at the promise and potential each life contained.

What other lives could you begin to lead from now on? Consider all the good parts of the lives you didn't choose before. What do you want to keep and what do you want to change? Remember, the habits and thoughts and things and people that have surrounded you in the past don't need to be there in the future. Step out of your comfort zone and into growth.

By noticing the choices you have made and the reasons for them, you can uncover old beliefs and values. You can get closer to understanding what's important for you now and make sure you don't sacrifice what you really want due to social conditioning.

EXERCISE: MY BIG BUCKET LIST

What to keep: What are the big things you are grateful for that you want to keep?

What to let go: What are the big things you no longer want in your life?

My big bucket list: What are the big, new things you want instead?

EXERCISE: THE THRESHOLD GUARDIAN

This final exercise taps into your imagination and instinct.

In many stories there is a character known as a threshold guardian. Think of the trolls in fairy tales who guard bridges, or the sphinx in ancient Egyptian and Greek mythology who posed riddles to travellers and devoured those who could not answer them. A threshold guardian is there to make sure you are really determined, resolved and ready for the next stage of your adventure. If you can get past them, then you will have an easier time on the next leg of your journey because you have a strong reason why to carry on. Imagine if the main character of the story had no will or resilience. How would he ever defeat Voldemort? How would Frodo Baggins survive the dark forces of magic standing in his way? How would Rapunzel escape from the tower? How would any main character ever move their life forward?

Perhaps you too have a threshold guardian who prevents you from doing things. Pause for a moment and imagine what they might be like. Now ask yourself: How ready are you to challenge the threshold guardian? Do you want to change the way you think about yourself? Would you like to break old habits and finally move through that personal plateau?

Imagine that you can talk to your threshold guardian. What do they sound like when they speak to you? How do they move? Make the image as real as possible. Now tell them why you want them to move aside and let you begin a new life.

If the guardian keeps pushing you back from the threshold, argue with them. Tell them forcefully to get out of your way, NOW!

EXERCISE: JOURNALLING

Begin a regular journalling practice. Use your journal to document your thoughts and to draw any pictures or images that come to mind. Or, if you prefer, you can use the space at the back of this book to write down your thoughts.

First thing in the morning is a great time to do this. Sit in a quiet place free from distractions and think about how you are feeling today and what aspect of your life you want to focus on. Write your thoughts down as they arise, without judging them or yourself. Just let your thoughts flow onto the paper, naturally and without effort. This is all about discovering your authentic voice: getting in touch with your subconscious to uncover feelings, dreams and beliefs. Keep everything you write; it will help you to reflect and review patterns and themes as you move through the seven steps.

'The past has no power over the present moment.'
Eckhart Tolle

GET READY FOR THE NEXT STEP

You're about to meet your mentor. Your mentor will offer you a choice – to make a wish and go on an adventure, or to refuse the call. Which will you choose?

No matter what's happening in your life, take a moment to celebrate. Rejoice at what is good and get ready to change everything else. You are about to take a road to new adventures and a truly satisfying existence. The past will soon be behind you. Now, you are standing at the edge of the cliff, ready to step towards the future of your dreams.

'Realise deeply that the present moment is all you have. Make the NOW the primary focus of your life.'

Eckhart Tolle

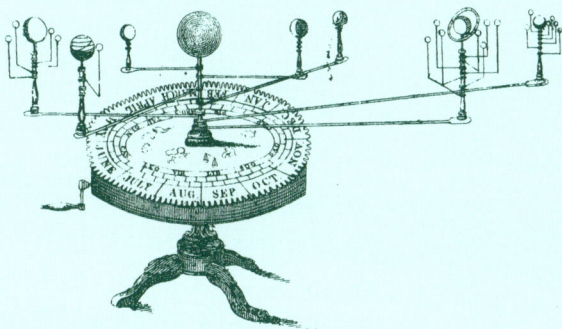

STORY: A SECOND CHANCE

Emily was a rising star in PR. In her twenties, she worked for several celebrities as a young public relations professional at a large company. She was successful not only because of her creativity and hard work but also due to her incredible ability to win clients. At just 29, she started her own company and began making even bigger money.

But as the business grew, so did the pressure. The money was rolling in, but Emily started relying on drinking to get her through the week. Just one glass of wine, then another. She justified it by telling herself it helped her build relationships with new and existing clients. However, drinking soon became a way of life, and the only reward she felt was the cash piling up in her account.

Of course, much of the money went out on designer clothes, gifts for friends and expensive holidays. But why not? She could afford it. The gifts were important – she often had to miss special occasions for family and friends because she was flying to Cannes, attending a music festival in the US with a client, or launching a film on the other side of the world.

She hardly noticed when her boyfriend dumped her because he complained about never seeing her. She was at the peak of her career.

Then one day, she woke up with a hangover in Monaco and realised it was three in the afternoon. She had missed her older sister's baby shower in London. She looked in the mirror and saw the loneliness in her eyes. The money and drinking couldn't mask the reality. For the first time, she called her sister, apologised sincerely, and admitted the truth about her drinking. Her sister listened and gently asked, 'What do you really want in your life?'

Emily flew back to Manchester, took some time off work, and started attending an alcohol support group. She also joined a workaholics group, where she met other women who had faced similar struggles. It was then she realised she had a second chance.

A year later, Emily had a very different life. She had sold her business and was training to become a therapist. Her finances were on track, and she had given herself time to explore what truly mattered to her. She knew her whole life was ahead of her, and was determined to keep manifesting these exciting changes.

STEP TWO:

THE WISH

'If you don't
know where
you're going,
you'll end up
someplace else.'

Yogi Berra

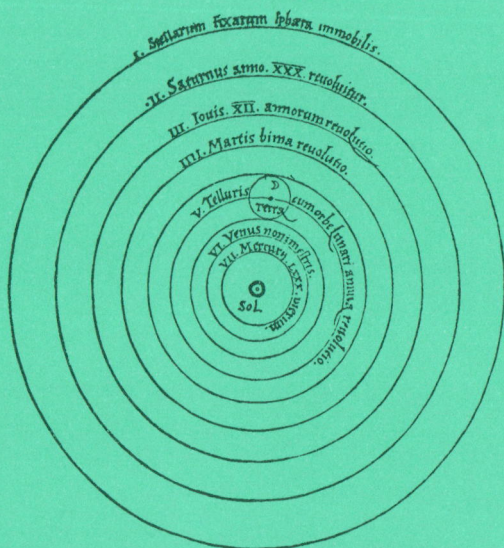

You are eager to move forward. In this second step, you will decide what you want and craft your first wish.

In the master story pattern, it is at this point that a mentor figure appears to help the main character move forward. Think of Gandalf in *The Hobbit* or the Fairy Godmother in *Cinderella*. In many myths, a god figure plays this role. Throughout this book, I will introduce you to different story characters like this because it's a great way of tapping into different resources within yourself. In this step, you will meet your own mentor figure.

'Dreams do come true, if only we wish hard enough. You can have anything in life if you will sacrifice everything else for it.'
J. M. Barrie, *Peter Pan*

As the author of your future, you are going to write out your wishes before you begin to live them. You've already considered this in the last step, but now you can build on this to reflect further on what you really want. Authentic wishes will align with your sense of purpose and true values. The universe has an infinite capacity to manifest ANYTHING for you, so let your imagination soar.

Reflect on what you truly love and are passionate about welcoming into your life. You can make a wish of any size: a sum of money, a new home, an offer to travel to an exotic location, or a promotion in your career. Experimenting with different sizes of wishes can help you become more and more confident in your abilities.

To manifest successfully, your wish must be compelling. Your wish should light up your spirit, fill you with excitement and come alive in your mind's eye when you visualise it. The joy, happiness and excitement associated with the picture of the wish should be as great as for a small child eagerly waiting to unwrap their presents on Christmas Day.

Only you can identify the right wishes for you. No one in existence will ever live the same life as you. Dwell on this idea for a moment. How do we measure success or failure in life? For every person who seems to be struggling, there is another who appears to have it all: money, family, love, a great career. In reality, we know nothing of other people's lives. Some lives seem glossy and glamorous on the surface, but underneath the façade are filled with misery. Others may appear small, dull or mundane to others, but in fact that person feels immensely satisfied and fulfilled. You get to decide what you want to wish for: small wishes that add glitter and sparkle to your life, or life-changing ones.

GETTING STARTED

If you are not sure about what your big wishes might be and just want to experiment, start by creating a little wish. You could wish for a particular sum of money, a holiday, or an experience. Here's a good wish you can practise to prove your abilities to yourself: parking spaces. I always wish for a parking space, and invariably a car moves away just as I'm approaching. Or I wish for an invitation for the weekend, and then someone rings. Occasionally, I wish for an amount of money I believe is achievable and it appears in my life in the strangest of ways. I once sold some antiques at auction. The estimate sale price was around £200. I wished for a thousand just for fun, and ultimately, I got £1200. Sometimes, a cheque appears out of the blue. This is the difference between manifesting and setting goals. The universe will surprise you with how it delivers.

If you are ready and want a big life transformation, I suggest that you think holistically about your future. Choose meaningful wishes. Later, you can create smaller manifesting milestones which will serve as stepping stones along the way. As an example of a big wish, a good friend of mine wished for a life spent saving animals in another country when she was young. It took ten years for her to get there. First, she moved across the world and taught English. Then she started helping a local vet for a few hours here and there. She rescued her first cat, and slowly became known as the animal lady. She was able to save all types of animals and eventually moved permanently overseas. Although she had no idea at first how the money would come, she met a local entrepreneur who gave her the money that she needed.

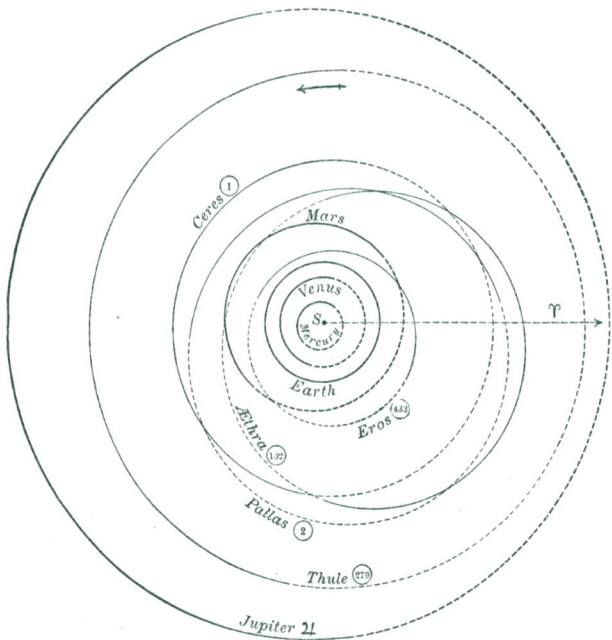

THE RULES OF MANIFESTING

You can wish for anything you want, as long as your
wish follows these rules:

1

It must be *do-able*, *be-able* and *have-able* by
someone. If it is, then you can do, be and have
it too. You must believe it is possible, not
necessarily probable.

2

It must be for you, not anyone else, because we can't
control other people.

3

It must be positively expressed, i.e. something you
do want, not something you *don't* want.

4

It must be ethical. In other words, it can't hurt you
or anyone else in the world. If it does, you're going
to get kicked right back by the universe.

5

A wish is an intention. You must be able to picture
yourself having it, doing it, being it, as clearly as if it
were a memory.

6

Your picture of what you want must be compelling
so you can pay attention to it.

7

What you are receptive to and expect to happen is
what you will create.

*'All we have to decide is what to do
with the time that is given us.'*
J. R. R. Tolkien, *The Fellowship of the Ring*

MEET THE MENTOR

In the master story pattern, the mentor is the
character who shows the main character how to
make a wish. He or she is often a wizard, witch or
other magical character. Visualising your personal
mentor is one way to bring your wishes to life.
Personally, I imagine my mentor as a traditional
magician figure, like the one who features in some
tarot card decks. He (or sometimes she) carries a
wand which represents
the ability to bridge the
gap between the different
worlds, bringing what is in
spirit into matter. He also
has tools representing the
four elements (the pentacle,
wand, sword and cup, which
stand for earth, fire, air and
water). He uses these tools
to create magical alchemy.

Ultimately the picture you make of your mentor is up to you. I want you to draw on your instinct to create a picture of a figure who symbolises help and magic. It's worth noting that these characters from myth and fairy tales are common to humanity. They occur in the collective consciousness. As a result, they have powerful energy you can tap into. Just like you did with the threshold guardian, imagine what this character sounds like, how they dress and how they move. It can help to draw or paint them. Sit quietly, or meditate, or go to a special place in nature and imagine them speaking to you. He or she is about to ask you a question.

EXERCISE: THE MASTER QUESTION

Your mentor asks you the (deceptively simple) Master Question: 'What do you want?'
What is the first thing that comes to your mind? Write it down.
Here's another way to ask the same question: 'What if you could have whatever you want?'

Write down any ideas that come to mind during the reflection and afterwards. It can help to do these reflections to music or while walking to get your ideas flowing. You can use a particular place or piece of music as a way of anchoring your picture of your mentor. Each time you repeat this action, you'll be able access their energies easily.

UNDERSTAND YOUR PERSONAL WHY

When it comes to manifesting, 'Why do I want this?' is a much more important question than 'How can I get it?' How your wish will manifest is up to the universe. A strong *why* makes your wish compelling. When I first began practising manifesting, I didn't understand why all my wishes didn't come true. Some wishes simply refused to manifest. Now, when I look back on some of those old wishes, I realise I didn't really want them at all. I thought I wanted them, but my subconscious knew better. It realised that I wasn't ready, because those wishes would have required me to change my life in ways I wasn't prepared for. My reasons for changing weren't as big or compelling as my reasons for not changing.

For your big wishes especially, reflect on why you want them. Then ask yourself: which of these wishes are non-negotiable for you? Which wishes do you want even if they take a long time to manifest? Which would you want even if they change other aspects of your life? These questions usually enable you to ditch some of your wishes and keep the important ones.

As soon as you're ready, begin to contemplate your heart's desire. What would truly transform your external and internal worlds? Note that this wish should not involve manipulation of others to love you or do your will. Negative wishes will create bad karma, while a positive wish for you also brings positive benefits to others.

You deserve to have your heart's desire. Once you believe this, you can begin to make life-changing wishes. Why not author the most awesome story you can imagine?

'Why fit in when you were born to stand out?'

Dr. Seuss

STEP TWO
RESOURCES:

CRAFT
YOUR
WISH

EXERCISE: A WHOLE LIFE'S WORTH OF WISHES

In this exercise you will build on the previous exercises to script your wishes for the best future you can imagine.

Take out a fresh sheet of paper or open your journal. Write today's date on the paper. Reflect on the bucket list you created in Step One. Now is the perfect moment to ensure your wishes are comprehensive. Whatever you manifest will affect all areas of your life, so it's crucial to consider how you want to live and who you want to become as you dream about what your future could be like. Read the suggestions below before you start if you feel you need some guidance.

※ Consider your health and well-being first. Good health is a foundation for a happy life. Describe how you feel in your body in the future. Imagine how grateful you are for amazing health. Imagine what your health enables you to do. Visualise every fibre and cell of your body radiating with good energy.

※ Now think about love. Who loves you and who do you love as future you? What does it feel like to have an abundance of love in your life? Where do you feel this love in your body? What does it look like to be surrounded by love?

※ What about money and abundance? What does it feel like to have abundant finances in your life? How are you seeing yourself using this money?

※ What kind of work and career is fulfilling for the future you? Perhaps you have changed career. Maybe you've achieved a promotion. Do you see yourself as an amazing entrepreneur, a great employee, boss or creative?

※ Where is your home? What is it like? Have you moved home? Moved overseas? Do you live in a small or large space? In the city or the countryside? How does the space inside and outside your home make you feel? What kinds of items are in your environment?

※ How does this life bring future you a sense of purpose and personal and spiritual growth? What has changed that means you are living an authentic life? See your life full of peace, connection and purpose.

※ Is there a contribution you are making to the people around you? Society? The world as a whole? Imagine positively impacting others and enriching the world now and in the future.

Now, without judgement, describe your future ideal life using the present tense. Think about all the areas of your life in which you would like to manifest: love, relationships, home, finances, career, personal development, friendships, travel, education and any others. Write down your wishes in the present tense, i.e. starting with 'I am', 'I own', 'I have', 'I am doing', and so on. This makes your wishes come alive.

EXERCISE: CREATE YOUR FIRST WISH

In this exercise you will consider again your motives and pick one wish you want to reinforce. This will be your first wish.

※ Using another clean sheet of paper, or your journal, write out the wishes you desire to manifest. You can't be too specific. Detail is key to success.

※ Pick a date in the future for each of your wishes. It could be one year, three years, five years or even 20 years. It's up to you.

※ Check that you believe each of these wishes is possible for you. Make sure that you believe you have given each wish enough time to manifest. Check that the timelines of all the different wishes fit together. Be ruthlessly honest with yourself. If something doesn't ring true, change the wish or change the timeframe.

※ Ask yourself, what is the value of this wish? How important is it to me that I manifest this in my life? Why?

※ Think about how your wishes align with your deepest potential. Your future needs to be compelling to manifest.

If you don't really want it, you're unlikely to get it.

You can have any of these wishes you want immediately. Which do you pick? Circle the wish that will make the biggest difference in your life – this is the one to start with. Once you have written one wish into your future, you can add others of any size.

EXERCISE: MANIFEST USING YOUR SENSES

In this exercise, you will make a compelling 'mental video' of your future, using four of your senses. To do this, picture your chosen wish as if it has already happened to you on the date you have written down. See yourself living life as a different version of yourself.

What will you see and hear in the moment you manifest this wish? Use a fresh sheet of paper and begin to write, describing the images that come to you using the present tense and as vividly as possible. What will it feel like to have this wish come true?

Let me give you an example: imagine that I want to manifest a beautiful home in the country with animals and a garden, and I want this to be with family and friends. I start by writing out a description of my new home, adding visual imagery, sounds, smells, physical sensations and finally emotions:

My house has five windows with white windowsills, stone walls, a front door that is painted red. At the front is a garden with plant beds on either side, filled with red and white roses. I can smell the flowers, and I can hear birds singing in the sky. There are trees behind the house leading to a pond and a small waterfall. When I open the red door, I walk through a blue-wallpapered hall into a beautiful yellow living area. I remember buying this house and I feel so good that I own it.

Next I develop this picture into a specific moment:

What I can see: As I walk into the yellow living area, I can see my family and friends gathered inside there. They are sitting on big, blue velvet sofas. There is a marble bar area where champagne is being served because we are having a party to celebrate this new home.

What I can hear: I can hear excited chatter and my favourite music in the background. My oldest child calls out my name and runs towards me. I can hear a sports car driving up outside.

What I can touch: I feel the soft wool of my son's sweater as I hug him. I pick up my champagne glass and it is cold and smooth in my grasp.

What I can smell: I can smell the jasmine scent of the candles that are lighting and the logs burning in the fireplace.

What I feel: As I touch my son's sweater and look around the room I feel a sense of love surging inside my body. I can feel it in my chest.

Finally: I hear myself shouting, 'I love my new home!'

See if you can come up with a powerful word or phrase to end your visualisation with so it impresses deep into your subconscious. The stronger the images and emotions, the easier it is for your brain to create this future memory.

EXERCISE: FREEZE FRAME

Once you've written out your defining moment, imagine you can freeze the image, like a photo. Step out of the frame and look at yourself inside it. Feel yourself lifting this photo frame into the air and placing it into the date you have chosen in your future. Your wish is now planted in the future.

It is very effective to see your life as a path from the past, through the present, and into the future. You can also get your mentor figure involved. Imagine them casting a spell with you, using their wand to impress your wish into your future timeline with their incredible power. As soon as you have done this, step back and let go. By creating your 'future memory', you have made your wish. Its fulfilment is waiting for you straight ahead.

'Without leaps of imagination, or dreaming, we lose the excitement of possibilities. Dreaming, after all, is a form of planning.'
Gloria Steinem

STAY THE COURSE

There is now a gap between your present and your future. The gap is filled with real-life experiences. Be certain that your wishes will manifest as you move along this new path. Remember, you can create or edit wishes anytime because you are the author of your destiny. What you envision you can bring into existence. The life you desire begins with the decisions you make today.

Pay attention to what's important. Act with intention and stay receptive. Keep journalling and writing down your thoughts daily to keep you on track.

'You are never too old to set another goal or to dream a new dream.'
C. S. Lewis

STORY: THE POWER OF A WISH

Hiromi loved being a mother, but the last thing she expected was to have twins. Now she had two daughters and a son, all under eight years old. She had taken some time off from her busy job in the innovation department of a large company that made products for beauty and well-being. She was afraid that if she spent too much time away from work she'd never get her career back, so she hired someone to help – someone who would pick up her older daughter from primary school and take the twins to and from nursery during the week.

Even with help, balancing work and motherhood was tough. Daily life was chaotic – there were breakfasts and dinners to make, emails to respond to, and soon there would be hobbies to take the children to as they got older.

She often wished that things would get easier. She daydreamed about what it would be like to work in a community where everyone shared the responsibility of raising children. One particularly hectic morning, she wished aloud, 'I wish I could share my kids!'

Soon after, she heard that one of her colleagues in marketing wasn't coming into the office anymore.

Curious, Hiromi found Ken by the water cooler. It turned out he wasn't leaving – he had an elderly mother with dementia and had managed to negotiate working from home. He was the first person in the company who was allowed to work fully remotely, outside of the main offices.

Empowered by his example, Hiromi went to see HR. At first, they were concerned she wouldn't be able to do her work effectively and support her team, but Hiromi was determined to make her wish at least partly come true. She managed to secure a trial period of three months working from home.

From there, things snowballed. While working out of a local café, she met a group of parents who all worked remotely and homeschooled their children. It turned out that homeschooling didn't mean sitting at home and teaching kids all day. The parents shared activities and took turns helping each other.

Hiromi embraced the homeschooling lifestyle with passion. She even invented a tool to help schedule activities and make life easier for parents. Ten years later, she has happy children and a thriving community to turn to for support – just as she had wished.

STEP THREE:

BEGIN YOUR NEW LIFE

'No darkness lasts forever. And even there, there are stars.'

Ursula K. Le Guin

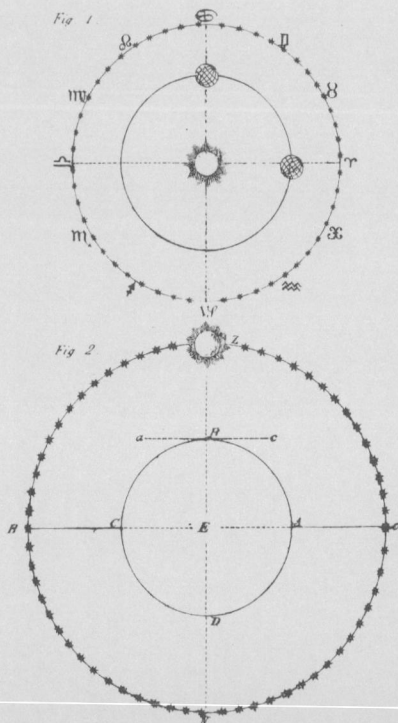

Fig 1

Fig 2

Congratulations! You have crossed the threshold. Your new story has begun. As soon as you create a future memory, your life immediately begins the process of changing. The universe is right now transforming your wishes into reality. With it, you are stepping away from the past and co-creating a new world. A new version of you will begin to emerge, like a butterfly breaking out from its chrysalis.

Right now, you may not be able to see much of the path towards your future life because it's under construction. But as you carry on paying attention to what you want to manifest and taking daily actions towards that end point, the path will begin to build itself, like a series of floor tiles being laid down in front of you. At times, you will only be able to see the tile you are standing on. At other times, you may get a glimpse of many tiles ahead.

This is the point in the story when the main character passes into a new realm. In *Alice's Adventures in Wonderland*, it is when Alice goes through the rabbit hole. In *The Wizard of Oz*, it's when the tornado transports Dorothy to the Land of Oz.

THE POWER OF ATTENTION

In this chapter, I'm going to introduce you to some concepts that will help you stay focused on your future. Every thought you ever have is like a seed planted in your subconscious mind. Some have been growing there since you were a small child. Many of those plants are well-tended now, and fresh seeds are bulking out the crop every day. Now you need to feed the seeds of your new life with three things: attention, intention and the expectation of success. Luckily, you don't just have your conscious mind to keep you on track; each time you programme a wish using the four senses method, your subconscious resources also jump into action.

'You have brains in your head. You have feet in your shoes. You can steer yourself in any direction you choose.'
Dr. Seuss, *Oh, The Places You'll Go!*

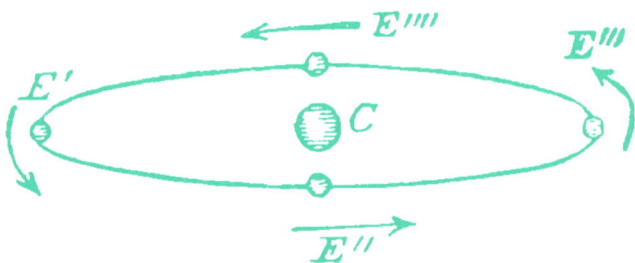

THE SCIENCE BEHIND MANIFESTATION:
How the brain decides what is important

Scientific research into memory shows that we are continually bombarded with sensory information every second of the day. Your brain is wired to forget more than 99 per cent of what you experience.

The answer is that the brain likes to remember things it deems important. It prioritises events that are novel, surprising and emotional over more mundane or ordinary events. This is why you focus on some thoughts and not others. It's also why some memories remain sharp and clear even after decades have passed.

How, then, do we decide what information to remember and register, and what information to forget and deprioritise? Human beings are very good at remembering significant events. You would be surprised if someone couldn't remember their wedding day or a major accident. So how does the brain highlight some events to make sure they become future memories? Your brain is working to ensure your wishes become future memories. Your wishes are now acting as a filter for your future life experience. As you follow the method in this book, your brain will automatically deprioritise all the experiences that will not help to manifest your wishes into reality. Because your brain is prioritising your well-being, it will help you to attract the circumstances that will help you to manifest your wish.

THE SCIENCE BEHIND MANIFESTATION:
Emotional tagging

Science calls the process of marking experiences in our brains 'emotional tagging'. Your brain – specifically the part of your brain known as your amygdala – determines which experiences are important enough to be transferred into long-term memory. However, the less relevant parts of these experiences do not get transferred. This means that the significantly emotional part of the event is safely stored away in your memory bank, while the rest is distorted or deleted.

If a memory has occurred near an event which aroused strong emotions, it will become an enduring memory. Other memories are still retained, but more selectively. It seems that often memories are retained and stabilised which fit around our identity and well-being. This applies as much to 'future memories' (i.e. your well-crafted wishes) as to past memories.

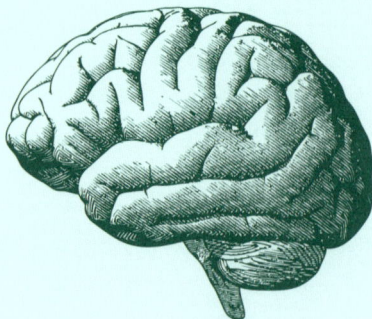

EMOTIONAL TAGGING
IN PRACTICE

When emotion tags an experience, it helps consolidate it into memory. Think back to the story you read in Step One, about my move to China when I was nineteen. In my first week there, everything I encountered was new – new sights, new sounds, new smells. It was also the first time I'd lived away from home without being able to contact my family, so my emotions were heightened. My brain naturally tagged this as an emotionally intense experience, which is why I still remember it so vividly today.

Emotional tagging works with both positive and negative experiences:

❋ I once had a close call with a potential phone thief in London. I was walking down the street, talking on my mobile, when a man on a bicycle suddenly lunged towards me to grab it. I managed to turn away just in time, and he missed. That memory remains crystal clear because it was emotionally charged. I also remember the street I was on – my brain wants me to remember it so I'll be more cautious if I ever walk that route again. It tagged the moment to help keep me safe.

※ Another time, I was working on a trading floor in Hong Kong when – just a week into the job – a client asked me to buy a million dollars' worth of a particular stock. I had only minutes to crunch the numbers and place the order before the price moved. Maths was never my best subject, and I felt a wave of panic. But then a memory surfaced: my first job, in institutional investment in Scotland, when a kind and supportive boss walked me through a similar trade. That experience had been tagged as positive, and in this high-pressure moment, it brought me clarity and confidence. My brain clicked into gear, and I got the job done.

These are both examples of how emotional tagging works with past experiences – but your brain is also capable of tagging future memories. When you attach strong feelings to a vision of the future, it signals to the brain that this is important and worth paying attention to. Your brain responds by helping you seek out experiences, cues and opportunities connected to that goal.

That's what you did in the exercise in Step Two: you pictured what you wanted and layered feelings onto that image. Those images are now stored in your brain as future memories, and your brain is already at work, scanning for ways to help make them a reality.

SAVOURING

When you have an experience you enjoy, your brain releases dopamine, a neurotransmitter involved in helping us feel pleasure. Increased dopamine activity can strengthen your ability to learn new skills and your desire to repeat them. Enjoying what you are doing by savouring the moment can lead to a spiral of positive emotions.

I loved my first job in institutional investment. Every day, it gave me a dopamine hit as I walked into work. I enjoyed the tasks I was doing, the people I was surrounded by, and even the historic building in the heart of Edinburgh where we were based. I looked forward to going to work every day and so I attracted good things into my life. By adding a feeling to your future memories when you visualise them, you release dopamine. Every time you pay attention to what you wish to manifest, your brain enjoys this effect.

GENERALISING

Generalisation allows us to adapt our behaviour to new situations. This can be negative or positive. For example, I might generalise that all streets are potentially full of mobile phone thieves and never go out again. Excessive

negative generalisation is going to interfere with you manifesting successfully. But positive generalisation is going to help you.

For example, I might, after one brief but enjoyable relationship, generalise that all future relationships will therefore be enjoyable and so actively pursue another one after the breakup. After learning something new, I might generalise that I love learning. After my first salary rise, I might generalise that I'm great at making money and therefore keep attracting it. Notice whether your generalisations for your future are positive or negative.

'People look for the meaning of life when actually they are looking for an experience of life.'
Joseph Campbell

WORLDBUILDING

Worldbuilding is the process of creating a fictional world with a unique history, geography, culture and other characteristics. Authors build worlds to make their stories more realistic and compelling. If you think about some of the stories you have read that really engaged you and that are still memorable today, it is likely that they all have rich, believable backdrops against which the plots unfold. If you were writing a fantasy epic, a thriller

THE AUTHOR'S ROLE

At this point, your story has a beginning and an ending, but you have only written a little bit of what comes between. So, what does an author have to consider when creating a vibrant story?

- ※ They must know their central character well.
- ※ They must know what the end of the story looks like.
- ※ They need to understand the main character's motivation to reach the end.
- ※ They need to know the internal world of the character, including all their flaws.
- ※ They must construct the external world – what kind of world will contain the story most effectively and propel the main character along on their journey? This includes thinking about who will help the main character on their path.

In storytelling, the main character meets many people along the way. Some turn out to be enemies, while others become mentors and friends. Who we choose to be in our lives has a big effect on us.

or a successful detective series, you would need to think about the location of the story, the type of people the main character is going to encounter in their adventures, and the customs and traditions of those people. Such stories win fans because they are immersive and detailed,

with well-thought-through rules and coherent and logical elements.

The typical kind of questions an author asks when worldbuilding are: what kind of world will produce the result our main character wants? How will this world differ from the worlds our main character has been part of before? What kind of people will help them along the way? Who will they outgrow? Who will inspire them? What kind of beliefs will they form as they journey through this new world? How will this new world change them?

When it comes to manifesting, worldbuilding involves creating the kind of world you want to live in, first in your imagination and then in your real life. By asking yourself these same kinds of questions, you will be congruent about your wishes. This will help your brain by allowing it to use all the mechanisms described above to guide you towards the things you want to attract. What you ultimately gain will have greater emotional impact.

'World building is not just about creating a place, but crafting a story that exists within it, giving life to its inhabitants and breathing soul into its landscapes.'
J. Edwards Holt, *The Seven Branches*

THE SECRET GARDEN,
Frances Hodgson Burnett

In this famous story written in 1911, Mary Lennox is a spoiled and lonely 10-year-old child. A cholera epidemic strikes, killing Mary's parents and leaving her an orphan. Mary is sent to live with her uncle at Misselthwaite Manor in Yorkshire, England. However, when she arrives her uncle is away, so she is left alone with the servants. The only servant who cares for her is kindly Martha Sowerby, who tells her something about her family and a mysterious locked garden.

Mary meets a robin who helps her finds the key to the secret garden, which once belonged to her aunt. As she begins to restore the garden with the help of Ben Weatherstaff, the gruff gardener, she makes new friends: Dickon, the brother of her maid, and Colin, a sickly cousin. These friendships are pivotal to changing Mary from a spoiled and isolated child into a kind, empathetic person. As she changes, so does the external world: the garden blooms and becomes beautiful once again. What's more, Colin mirrors Mary's transformation as he too becomes healthier the more time he spends in the garden.

Just as Mary's transformation is reflected in the growth of the garden, so too will your transformation be mirrored by your own external world.

STEP
TOWARDS
SUCCESS

Use the exercises in this section to contemplate your new world.

EXERCISE: WORLDBUILDING

How real does your future world look to you? When you intentionally act like the person who can have this new life, your brain begins to believe that you are becoming a different person. You can create any change you want to if you act consistently in alignment with this new identity, because your new identity is true to who you really are.

Say to yourself, '*I am not _____ anymore. Instead, I am _____.*' See what is revealed to you.

Describe again on paper what your new world will look like with your wishes realised. I want you to pay attention to the environment and context in which your wishes will be manifested. What will have changed in your external world? You can take a fresh sheet of paper and draw images of your new world, or fill a vision board with more motivational pictures of your future life. If you choose to make a vision board, make sure you place it somewhere in your home where you will see it regularly.

Recently I've been enjoying making pictures using AI. I made a series of pictures of a wedding day for a friend, feeding in the ideal environment and physical characteristics of the bride and

groom. Imagine the life you will live on the journey to your future memory, when you have lived your future memory, and what happens next.

As the author of your own future, the better you can imagine the future world you would like to manifest, the more control you will have over your own destiny. While you may have thought about some of the questions below when you encoded your wish, in my experience, revisiting them sparks new ideas and new details.

Jot down the answers to these questions below:

※ What kind of person are you in your new life? What do people like about you? What are your beliefs? What legacy is your life likely to leave?

※ What do you gain from this new life? What has changed for you? What will you leave behind? What have you resolved from the past that has enabled you to move forward?

※ Who loves you and who do you love?

※ Do you foresee any challenges that might sabotage you? What must you change in your world to minimise these?

※ Think about your daily life and environment. What type of people do you meet daily? What shops do you go to? What's your home like? How much money is in your bank account? Do you have an office? What are you known for in your career? What colours are in your home? Where do you travel

to? What time of day do you get up and go to sleep?
Do you have pets? A partner? Children? Do you follow a
spiritual tradition or have political beliefs? What food do
you eat? What kind of exercise do you do?

*'To hear the voice of the silence is to understand
that from within comes the only true guidance.'*
Mabel Collins

EXERCISE: AMPLIFY GOOD FEELINGS

This exercise helps you to programme your subconscious by
flooding your future memories with positive feelings.

❋ Relax and think about a time when you successfully
   manifested something you really wanted in your life. What
   happened and what did it feel like? Imagine that feeling right
   now. This is the feeling of success.

❋ Now think about what you have wished for and
   deliberately amplify that feeling. Imagine the wish being
   fulfilled, name the feeling you want to have and imagine the
   feeling coming into your body and growing stronger and
   stronger. If it helps, see a dial and turn the dial up to the
   max. Each time you do this, your subconscious has more
   reason to help you to successfully manifest.

※ Imagine you can bring in this feeling and amplify it every time you make a wish or think about your future world. The more positive feelings you generate inside your body, the more you will attract positive experiences using the perfect force of the law of attraction.

EXERCISE: JOURNAL

Spend some time reflecting regularly on your life to come and write your reflections in your journal, or in the journalling section in the back of this book. Think about how it feels to have this amazing new life. Imagine the dialogue between you and others as if you really are an author writing a script for the future you.

EXERCISE: ADD MUSIC

Experiment with creating an association between the music you love and the picture of your future memory.

※ Put on some music – a favourite song or album. It should be something you love, something that fills you with positive feelings. (I tend to prefer classical music without lyrics, as often your subconscious will listen to the message in the lyrics rather than paying attention to your memory. Most Mozart works brilliantly for me.)

※ Sit with closed eyes.

※ Bring your focus to the spot between your eyebrows –

this is your third eye. See your third eye opening up.

☀ Now imagine projecting the picture of your desired and realised picture through your third eye and onto a screen in front of you.

☀ Repeat this exercise regularly. When you play the music again, your brain will connect it to your manifested wish.

'Good writing is supposed to evoke sensation in the reader – not the fact that it is raining, but the feeling of being rained upon.'

E. L. Doctorow

STORY: ABUNDANCE IN EVERYTHING

Max seemed to have everything he could ever want in life. He had a designer apartment in the city, a six-figure salary, and plenty of friends. When he travelled, he always turned left into business class. His future seemed assured with a large pension.

But Max was consumed by fear. It had all come too easily. He was only 28, and there were already rivals snapping at his heels. He worried that his performance might not be as good as people perceived. What if this was the day he slipped up and said the wrong thing to a client? What if his job was taken from him? Would he ever be able to recreate this life again? What's more, did any of it matter without a life partner? Many of his colleagues had the career and a family, too, while Max was single. Even if he kept his career, how would he ever find a partner when he worked so hard? Who would want him?

Max came from a family where there was always anxiety about money. He had never known his father, and his single mother had struggled to bring up two children alone. He was haunted by the idea that he would lose everything and be the same as his mother, struggling from paycheque to paycheque. At the same time, he didn't trust others, which made it difficult to form relationships. He had a scarcity mindset. Abundance was for other people – not for him.

Max prayed for something to change. One evening at his local bar, he bumped into an old friend. The friend suggested that Max volunteer with him on Sundays at the local nursing home. Max agreed, and through his volunteer work with the older residents, he gradually came to the realisation that true wealth was about living life well, not just about money. One day Max took the plunge and joined a dating agency, where he met several potential partners who valued him not for his money and success, but simply for himself. Gradually, as his life shifted over several years, Max left his anxieties behind. He dumped the flashy car and apartment, met and married the love of his life, and manifested a house which he loves. Now that Max takes the time to enjoy life, he sees that it is full of riches.

STEP FOUR:

HELP IS HERE

'Grown-up people
find it difficult
to believe really
wonderful things,
unless they have what
they call proof. But
children will believe
almost anything…'

E. Nesbit

Now you are well on your way to manifesting. Perhaps some of your smaller wishes have manifested quickly and you are now in the process of creating bigger wishes. With every wish, little by little, you are becoming a new person. You have powerful resources to draw on.

Harry Potter had Hermione and Ron, Hagrid, Dumbledore, Sirius Black and many other friends and allies to help him. Bilbo Baggins had the dwarves, Gandalf the Grey and the elves of Rivendell. Alice was befriended in Wonderland by the Cheshire Cat, the Gryphon and the Mouse. Luke Skywalker's friends Han Solo, Leia Organa, Chewbacca, C-3PO, and R2-D2 assisted him in defeating the Empire. Friends are a feature of these stories to show us that help is always here and will keep you on your path.

The main character in every great story has friends and allies who are vital in helping him or her along the path to their reward. We are deeply connected at every level with everything else on this planet. In your new world, mentors will develop you, and friends will help you to overcome tests and challenges. As you begin to attract new experiences and manifest different circumstances in your external world, you will automatically attract new people. In fact, this is a sign from the universe that you're on the right track.

'Seek the way by retreating within.
Seek the way by advancing
boldly without.'

Mabel Collins

YOUR EXTERNAL FRIENDS

Let's start with the outer world. It's important to be your own cheerleader on your new path, but friends are vital, too. The people who you choose to surround yourself with will either support you in manifesting effectively or block your path. The right people will share your new values and applaud your successes.

Not everyone will be willing or able to come on the same journey as you. Many people are afraid of a friend who is changing. Some will be jealous of your good fortune, while others will try to keep you in a familiar pattern of living or thinking because they feel safer if you don't leave your familiar set. But if there are people in your life who don't approve, then it's time to leave them behind and find a new tribe.

If you look at the people around you, you can intuitively sense that some of them are lighter than others. On an energetic level, this lightness can be called 'good vibrations'. Heavy, depressed people are not as light vibrationally. If your vibration is heavy, you will automatically attract similar people and experiences. If you want to understand your unconscious beliefs and patterns, just look at the issues your friends have. You magnetise people with the same mindset towards you. By raising your vibration and starting to eliminate negative thinking, different people will come into your orbit. This begins to happen automatically as you become more aligned with your authentic self.

I remember once meeting a group of people who were all divorced and had 'problem' children. They all shared common views about marriage which were negative. I realised straight away that I had nothing in common with them and, sure enough, they fell out of my orbit.

THE SCIENCE BEHIND MANIFESTATION:
The ripple effect

Who we choose to surround ourselves with has enormous consequences. When you are very young, you will naturally take on the beliefs and values of your family, but as we get older we are all influenced by the people around us. Thinking is contagious, values are contagious, and the way you see the world is influenced by the people in your life now, and those who were in your life in the past.

It's vital to be 100 per cent clear on *why* you want to manifest your wishes, because you are going to leave many things behind to create space for new things and people.

There are three different ways in which values and behaviours are spread. The first is known as 'social contagion', which means we change our views to fit in with a social group: this often includes authority figures. The second, 'behavioural contagion', is when we mimic or adopt the behaviours of others, often without realising we are doing it. The third way is called 'emotional contagion', and this is when we 'catch' emotions from others. Mimicking a friend's body language or facial expressions can help you feel their emotions and build closeness.

YOUR INTERNAL FRIENDS

Let's now explore your internal friends. Each of us is made up of a variety of behaviours and beliefs that shape our identity. We often say things like, 'part of me wants X, but another part wants Y'. When we say this, it's a sign that our subconscious is in conflict with itself. One part of us holds certain beliefs, values or intentions that may conflict with other parts of our self. Some of these parts help us get where we want to be, and some stand in the way of change.

A *sabotaging* part of you is one that, despite wanting the best for you – such as keeping you safe or preventing harm – ends up getting in the way of your success. For example, you might have a 'hard-working' part that drives you to pursue promotions and earn money, but you may also have a 'sabotaging' part that causes you to drink too much when you do earn money. Or perhaps you have a part that's great at losing weight, but another part that resists because a heavier you feels safer from unwanted attention.

Archetypes are recurring characters found in myths, stories and life. You have already met the mentor, the threshold guardian and the fool. Each archetype is characterised by a set of behaviours and traits. We relate to archetypes because they are universal. The stories we

read about them simply illustrate how they interact with different situations.

Have a look at this list and see which of the archetypes you most recognise in yourself and in the stories you have read.

1. THE MAGICIAN

The mentor is also often called the magician. The magician is not necessarily an old man. In the tarot, he is a much younger man with golden hair. Sometimes he has a beard to symbolise wisdom. Sometimes the magician is a woman, like the fairy godmother in *Cinderella*. This archetype's energy allows you to access your inner will and ability to manifest on any new path you take.

Think of the image you created earlier. Which is the part of you that is closest to the energy and resources of a magician? What does this part of you do for you?

2. THE SAGE, OR THE WISE MAN

The sage is wise, logical and calm. This archetype is generally portrayed as a man with a beard, but of course as a woman you can still access the essence of this archetype within you; all of us have access to male and female energies. The sage may have magical powers, but he uses these with restraint and mentors by using his wisdom and emotional intelligence. Obi Wan Kenobi,

Yoda, Merlin, Dumbledore and Gandalf are all examples of the sage. This archetype's energy allows you to access your inner wisdom in times of trouble.

3. THE RULER

The ruler exudes power, strong masculine energy and authority. The ruler commands a kingdom or empire and expects respect and obedience. They love structure, so they take well to order and habit. A good ruler looks after his subjects with compassion and bravery, remaining calm under pressure. This is a modern CEO or COO archetype. Shakespeare's King Henry V is a classic example of a strong ruler archetype, as is Mufasa in *The Lion Ling* and President Snow in *The Hunger Games*. This archetype's energy provides the ability to pursue a new direction and decline requests from those who may impede your progress. How useful would it be for you to draw on this energy to stand your ground as you build your new world?

4. THE REBEL

The rebel stands up against authority. They take a different path, even if society disapproves. He or she is willing to fight their corner and be disruptive if they think it is necessary to get a result. They are passionate, fearless and ready to make a change and create a lasting

impact. We love stories about people who take their own paths, and you'll see examples of this archetype everywhere – Han Solo in *Star Wars*, the Scarlet Pimpernel, Katniss Everdeen in *The Hunger Games*, and, of course, Robin Hood. You can connect with this archetype when you are ready to challenge the status quo and need the impetus to take your own path.

5. THE WARRIOR

The warrior has a similar kind of energy to the rebel. The warrior is an expert fighter who can see off any enemy. They are driven to be courageous in all their actions. They will fight battles and slay dragons. They are competent and active in taking on challenges and facing and overcoming ordeals. How active has this part been within you?

6. THE CAREGIVER

This archetype helps other people. They are loving and nurturing. Often, they are parent figures, guardians, or even kind bosses who fulfil a parental role. They will put themselves out to help others, and are empathetic, selfless or altruistic. One example of the caregiver from literature is Beth in *Little Women*, who is always trying to help, often at her own expense. Another is the much-loved fictional character of Mary Poppins.

Many us who find it hard to say no have a bit too much caregiver energy, which can turn into putting others before ourselves. If this sounds like you, try tapping into your inner ruler instead from time to time.

7. THE CREATOR

This archetype can provide you with extra energy when you lack imagination and get stuck. This archetype is curious and inventive – think of Sherlock Holmes or Dr Frankenstein. They're visionary and bold, often coming up with new solutions to old problems. They believe that if it can be imagined, then it can be created.

When you get stuck for a new idea, turn to this friend for inspiration – open up your journal and write down what comes to you. It can be helpful to use a mind map structure to encourage the ideas to flow.

8. THE HERO

Finally, there is the hero archetype: brave, individual, risk-taking, sometimes a little foolhardy. Think of King Arthur, Joan of Arc, Mulan. Just like the fool, the hero initially exhibits traits of naivety, but they develop maturity and courage as the story unfolds.

HOW TO USE YOUR ARCHETYPES

It can be helpful to start by thinking about which archetypes you relate to most. This can give you a clue about what energies you use to relate to other people. Every archetype is already part of us, but while we have been great friends with some parts of ourselves since childhood, we have barely got to know others.

Every archetype, when overused, can be too much of a good thing. Perhaps you are strongly connected to your ruler energy but not your creator energy. Maybe you overuse caregiver energy and don't relate to your inner rebel. Just remember, nothing in you has been created to be a destructive influence on your life. Your subconscious is always trying to do the best it can for you.

In the resources section you will learn how to access these different personalities to support the identity you want for the new world you are building. The more you learn to relate to them, the more you can call upon them when in a tight spot. For example, you can call on your creator energy when you are stuck for ideas, or your ruler energy when you need to be assertive, or your hero energy when you just need to keep going through challenge after challenge.

LIFE OF PI
Yann Martel

This bestselling book aligns beautifully with the master story pattern. Pi Patel lives a peaceful life in Pondicherry, India, until his family decides to emigrate to Canada due to political instability. Pi is reluctant to leave his familiar life behind in India. However, he sets forth on a boat. There is a shipwreck, and Pi is stranded with his mentor, a Bengal tiger, from whom he receives guidance. Pi faces challenges, including storms, hunger and the need to tame the tiger. He finds a floating island which he could stay on, but realises that this isn't the solution. His great ordeal comes when he is near starvation. His bond with the tiger helps him to survive. Finally, Pi finds his reward, surviving the journey and gaining spiritual insight from his ordeal.

STEP FOUR
RESOURCES:

LEARN
AND
EVOLVE

'If you always put limits on everything you do, physical or anything else, it will spread into your work and into your life. There are no limits. There are only plateaus, and you must not stay there, you must go beyond them.'
Bruce Lee

EXERCISE: GET TO KNOW YOUR ARCHETYPES

In this exercise, you will get to know your own archetypes better. Start with what you consider to be your most dominant archetype.

In your journal or on a fresh sheet of paper, write a description of this archetype as you see them. Describe them physically. Perhaps they have a name already, or perhaps now a name comes to you. Think about the clothes they wear, what their movements are like. Where do they sit in your body? How big or small are they? The more you can connect with them the better. See them in your mind's eye. Imagine them moving. Is there a sound connected with them? Make the sound out loud. Make this picture as vivid in your mind as possible. You can even draw your character if it helps.

Here's an example of what you might write about one of your archetypes.

My ruler is a king who is about 30 years old. He is called Harold.
He wears an ermine-trimmed, jade-coloured gown and sits on
a gold throne. He carries a sceptre and wears a crown full of
sparkling diamonds. He has dark, intelligent eyes and clear skin.
He has a kind and authoritative expression on his face. He wears
an emerald pendant around his neck. He moves slowly. He has a
deep voice, and when he speaks it is as powerful as the roar of a
lion. I feel his presence in my chest as a strong pulsing sensation.
He says the words, 'I command!'

Now get the feeling in your body as you access the
archetypal energy. If you are not sure how to do this, imagine
where the character might feel their inner power in their
own body and feel it in the same place in yours. Say the words
your archetype would say in the way they would say them, for
example, *'I command!'* in a powerful voice.

Once you have done this, break this connection by
thinking about a neutral image, for example, a cup of coffee.
Notice the difference between the neutral feeling in yourself
versus the archetypal feeling. Cycle through this a few times,
moving from the archetype to the neutral state so you feel just
how powerful this change is and how you perceive it in your
body. The more you do this, the easier you will find it to access
and build the power of each archetype.

Once you have done this exercise for your most dominant archetype, start building visual pictures and powerful feelings for all the archetypes.

STORY: A TALE OF EXPECTATION AND RECEPTIVENESS

Maddy, a British friend of mine, grew up in a disadvantaged area in the North of England. It was her dream that one day she would run a business empire. There is no way she could have known everything she would have had to do along the way, but she kept her faith and learned as she went along, and the universe rewarded her.

Maddy had always loved stories, especially detective tales. She devoured everything from Sherlock Holmes to Agatha Christie. She told me that whenever she faced a problem, she would imagine what Sherlock or one of the other detectives she admired would do to resolve it. How might they view the issue from a different angle, and how could they come up with an original solution? Though she didn't realise it at the time, Maddy was tapping into the classic energy of the creator archetype – exactly what she needed to resolve challenges.

In the 1990s, Maddy became a huge fan of *The X-Files* and related to the trailblazing, sceptical and intelligent heroine, Dana Scully. Scully embodies the feminist hero archetype in a professional context. She's not just a sidekick but a strong, central character – just the energy Maddy needed to channel in the competitive commercial world. In fact, Maddy still talks about calling on her 'inner Scully' whenever she needs to feel strong and is about to take a risk.

Fifteen years after she took out her first loan and purchased her first property, Maddy headed up a very successful property business. But it wasn't just her material wishes that came true. Maddy always says that she saw herself being content and happy in her future in a way she and her family weren't when they were growing up. She has grown into the person she always dreamed of becoming. The tests and trials the universe sent her taught her to be a new person – a happy person.

YOU ARE TESTED

'Your beliefs become your thoughts, your thoughts become your words, your words become your actions, your habits become your values. Your values become your destiny.'

Attributed to Gandhi

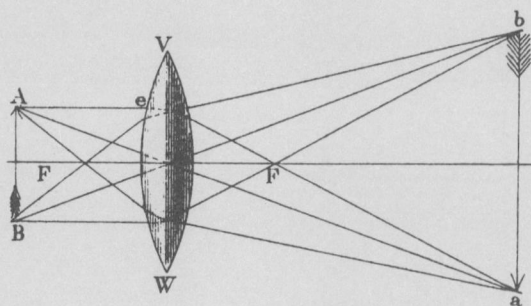

In every great story there are enemies to overcome and obstacles to conquer. Think about all the fairy stories, myths and legends which have stayed with you all these years. The main character in every one of them will have to overcome a barrier at some point in the story. Great stories which endure over the centuries are also teaching tools. They remind us that every human being faces common experiences in their lifetimes. Dorothy in *The Wizard of Oz* faces the field of poppies, the dark forest and the Wicked Witch. Hansel and Gretel must escape the clutches of the evil witch.

We all get tested. Do you often fail to get what you really want? Do you repeat patterns of behaviour so the same circumstances occur in your life again and again? The only thing that can get in the way of successful manifesting is you – the old you. The you from the ordinary world with the old thoughts. As the author of the next part of your life, you can change this forever.

'Obstacles don't have to stop you. If you run into a wall, don't turn around and give up. Figure out how to climb it, go through it, or work around it.'
Michael Jordan

As you transition to your new life, encountering some obstacles is inevitable. Some of these are minor. Others

may seem insurmountable at first glance. Fortunately, no obstacle is meant to bring a full stop to your plans. The universe brings tests to check your intentions. You can keep examining your identity, refining your story and overturning unhelpful beliefs. This is where the master story pattern serves us well. It reminds us that apparent chaos can be transformed into something hopeful, enlightening and profound.

In the master story pattern, when the reward seems lost the main character discovers the inner strength to overcome whatever stands in the way. An obstacle is just a chance to dig deeper, to discover inner resilience, character and courage. Every challenge overcome is a moment to celebrate the transformation occurring within you and magnetising your reward closer. Even when realising your wishes seems impossible, maintaining your faith will transform you into an unstoppable force, making you wiser and stronger.

'Liking the person we go on a journey with is the single most important element in drawing us into the story.'
Blake Snyder, *Save the Cat*

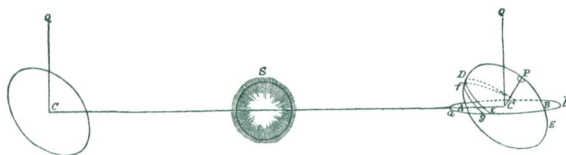

HOW TESTS APPEAR

Your tests and obstacles, like your friends and enemies, appear in both the internal and external world. As you are now aware, there is no separation between the two. One is a mirror to the other. Notice when unwanted thoughts and emotions appear in your internal world. These may emerge just as you begin to align your life with your manifestation goals, as if deliberately trying to derail your progress. At the same time, in your external world you may find you attract unwanted people or circumstances.

You're naturally more open to receiving certain blessings from the universe. Conversely, you may find unconscious resistance to some types of change in your life. This disparity in manifestation is a normal part of the process. You might not have anticipated all the consequences of changing yourself internally or altering your external world. If your subconscious is not convinced that fulfilling your wishes is beneficial, it will refuse to let you manifest 'for your own good'. Old patterns are revealed. Your intention, attention and expectation are going to be tested again and again. But these tests can only get in the way if you choose to let them. This is your story, and you are its author.

'Each of us has the power to enter a new world. All we have to do is change our mind.'

Matt Haig

OLD PATTERNS ARE REVEALED

This is how it happens: your wishes are about to come true. You can see your life changing around you. They are so near you can almost touch them and you can sense them about to materialise. And then what happens? Out of nowhere, an old pattern appears.

Say, for example, that you fall in love. You think that this person is 'the one', and then the dynamics of the relationship change. You realise that this new relationship is just like all the others you had – which is not what you wanted to manifest at all. Or perhaps you wanted to manifest a beautiful home in the countryside where you could have peace and quiet. As you pick up the keys, the agent tells you about the new 100-home estate that's about to be built next door.

WHAT'S GOING ON?

When these negative factors get in the way of your positive wishes, you're being tested by the universe to see if you are congruent about what you want. Your conscious mind may want the loving relationship, or the beautiful home in the countryside, but your subconscious is not so sure it's the best thing for you. Whenever a challenge arises, take a moment to ensure that your wishes are still perfectly aligned with your desired end outcome. Reflect on your genuine beliefs about whether you truly deserve to have your wishes realised.

'Midway upon the journey of our life
I found myself within a forest dark,
For the straightforward pathway had been lost.'
Dante, *The Divine Comedy*

'When you feel fear about taking a risk, hit the
pause button, not the stop button.'
Ben Hunt-Davis, *Will it Make the Boat Go Faster?*

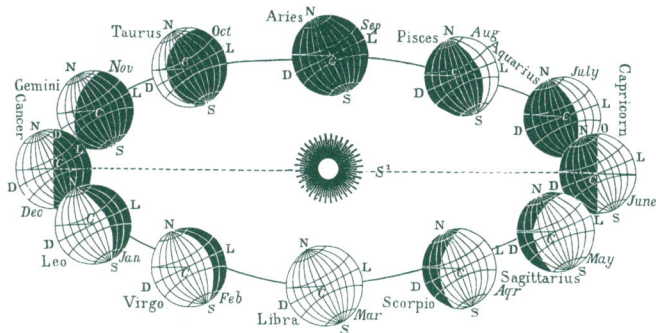

THE SCIENCE BEHIND MANIFESTATION:
Emotional hijacking

Your new path in life will attract new situations – after all, this is what you wished for. So why, then, do you sometimes feel overwhelmed with negative emotions? What's happening? It's called 'emotional hijacking'. The term 'emotional hijacking' was coined by the author Daniel Goleman. In his writing on emotional intelligence, Goleman explains that certain situations will trigger negative emotions, which in turn can lead to emotional flooding. When you experience this, it's because the amygdala – the part of your brain which processes emotions – has taken control. Before that occurs, the prefrontal cortex – which is responsible for logical thinking – is running things. The amygdala is fast, so it can feel like the emotions are pouring in out of nowhere. Suddenly you feel stressed, out of control and derailed from your normal way of thinking and acting. If this happens to you, be grateful to your subconscious; it is revealing your old patterns. Emotions can be triggered when you encounter situations that remind you of something in the past that you haven't dealt with. These emotions are a clue to your true perspective on life. They signal that your mindset is not yet flexible enough to cope with your changing reality – and they often point to unconscious beliefs. Once you've identified these unconscious beliefs, you can begin to ask yourself:

What would I *rather* believe instead? Then, visualise what your life could look like if you were empowered by these new beliefs. This process will help you shift your mindset and manifest a more positive outcome.

THE BELIEF–EXPECTATION CONNECTION

If you tend to home in on negative experiences and have anxiety about potential problems, it's likely you hold deep-seated beliefs that reinforce this perspective. These create a fixed mindset, which can stop you from manifesting. Your subconscious may prefer you to get attention because you are a 'victim', rather than no attention because you are 'successful', perhaps because victimhood has produced more friendships in the past. If this is you, drill down. It's possible to change this mindset. Ask yourself, 'Does every part of me believe I can get what I want?' Be ruthlessly honest. If you can't articulate the hidden limiting beliefs, pay attention to your emotions. What would be a life which would allow me to have *everything* I want?

THE SCIENCE BEHIND MANIFESTATION:
The Conscious Critical Faculty

In psychology, the Conscious Critical Faculty (or CCF) is a mental mechanism which acts as a kind of protective gatekeeper between the conscious and subconscious minds. The CCF protects you from information and ideas that contradict your existing beliefs, values and experience. Basically, it doesn't want you to be exposed to ideas that might conflict with your sense of identity and so it compares new information it encounters to your old beliefs and your existing knowledge. You can think of it rather like the firewall or anti-virus package you get with your computer, or like your lens on life.

You might wonder why this exists. Consider ancient humans: they needed to be able to make very fast, 'instinctual' decisions. If you saw a wild animal coming at you, ideally you wouldn't just sit around wondering what to do. Your subconscious needed to be able to make a fast assessment of whether you were able to fight or whether it was better to take flight.

'If you have good thoughts they will shine out of your face like sunbeams and you will always look lovely.'
Roald Dahl, *The Twits*

THE CCF IN PRACTICE

The CCF doesn't have a concept of good or bad, but it pushes away anything it feels might be a threat to your sense of who you are. It helps you to make decisions consistent with your current identity. Like a firewall, it has your best interests at heart, trying to help you to survive in a world full of complex information. If you lack sufficient positive feelings towards your future memory, and if your current beliefs conflict with your wishes, then the CCF will shout, 'No, you can't have this new life, it's a threat to your nice, safe previous identity.'

The CCF is enormously helpful – unless you are actively trying to form a new identity. Then it can be very unhelpful, because it will reinforce your current limiting beliefs in order to keep the status quo.

Imagine this situation. Maisie wishes for a new life with a job promotion. She creates a vivid picture of herself in charge of her team. She thinks she has a compelling goal. But the emotion attached to the end picture isn't strong enough. She has always had a

nagging belief that she isn't good enough or intelligent enough to manage this level of responsibility. She is looking forward to the promotion to come, however, she gets some feedback from her boss that her project wasn't good enough. The CCF registers the feedback as true because it tallies with Maisie's existing beliefs about herself. However much she consciously wishes for the promotion, she also needs to take active steps to disprove these long-held beliefs. The CCF acts faster than the conscious mind, instantly blocking her from manifesting her wishes. Maisie doesn't see this, however; she simply sees the evidence in the external world that her promotion does not manifest.

Thankfully, there are ways to resolve this. By creating truly compelling wishes and feeling them coming true, the emotion attached to your future memory can squash old beliefs. Then, when you break free from your old patterns, you'll notice immediately; the external world will present you with new experiences, people and rewards, confirming that your internal world has been transformed.

'You're braver than you believe, stronger than you seem, and smarter than you think.'
A. A. Milne, *Winnie the Pooh*

NEGATIVE EMOTIONS

Let's name all the negative emotions that can block you.

FEAR

Fear is a primal human emotion that evolved in order to protect us from danger. It prepares us for fight or flight in response to an immediate threat. But it can also be shaped by childhood experiences, including picking up on your parents' anxieties, as well as through traumatic events. Fear is a powerful blocker to change, but it should never become a reason for you to prevent yourself from fully experiencing life. I was brought up hearing the very British expression, 'I'm afraid', as in, 'I'm afraid I can't help you', or 'I'm afraid I don't know'. In this context it simply means 'sorry' or 'no', however, imagine the effect on the subconscious of constantly hearing the words 'I'm afraid'? It was only later as an adult that I realised what a negative effect it had on my worldview.

HATE

Hate is another big emotion. Hate can come in two forms: hate for others, and self-hate. However, even when the emotion is projected towards an external person or situation, the emotion is still in *your* physical body. The person you hate may never care as much as you do, and ultimately, the person who really suffers is you. What's more, hate keeps you in a victim state, because it is triggered by the idea that someone or something else is responsible for bad things happening to you. This is a big blocker for manifesting as it gives control of your future to an external force.

ANGER

Anger can reveal itself to you in times of stress. Anger comes from the desire to punish others or yourself. When you are angry, your energy gets directed away from focusing on the light at the end of the path and towards side issues. This is a huge waste of your emotional energy. Even if you feel that someone else is to blame for a challenge in your life, you won't resolve it by being angry. The message of anger to the universe is, 'I am a victim', while the right manifesting message is, 'I can overcome any obstacle and carry on along the path'.

JEALOUSY

If you are jealous, it means that you are not grateful for what the universe has given you and you don't believe an abundant universe will reward your wishes. Jealousy is a powerful block to manifesting because it comes from a scarcity mindset. You may believe that someone else has more than you, or that they obtained what they have without effort, while you have had to try harder. Listen to the beliefs that lie behind the jealousy and you will uncover deep blocks. Often there is a belief that you don't deserve what others have, or that you will always have to work harder than they do to achieve it. On the other hand, the beliefs behind abundance are 'I can have anything', and 'I am pleased when others get what they want. Being surrounded by happy, fulfilled, rich people shows that my universe is abundant.'

'To love someone else is easy, but to love what you are, the thing that is yourself, is just as if you were embracing a glowing red-hot iron: it burns into you and that is very painful.'

Carl Jung, *Nietzsche's Zarathustra*

THE POWER OF LOVE

Love is the most powerful emotion in the universe. It creates an abundance mentality. It can overcome any obstacle. A victim mentality, hate and fear can only grow when there is a lack of self-love. All the love you project outwards to others will come back to you, because love is channelled through you.

Energy follows intention. If you intend to fill yourself with love, love will fill you up. If you want to feel more loved, just intend to notice the love around you and magnetise it to you. You don't have to heal anything, because you aren't broken. We would never think of a baby as lacking something, needing healing or being imperfect, and yet we project those very same thoughts onto adults.

Banish old disempowering thoughts by deliberately seeing in your mind's eye your body full of love channelled from the universe. Try this visualisation: imagine love flowing into the top of your head as a white light, filling up every cell of your body. Then see this light flowing out of your heart and filling up your room, reaching everyone you know, every situation in your life, and finally the whole world. You will feel amazing after just a few minutes of doing this.

Even in moments when you don't feel loved, it doesn't mean that love isn't there. It's like entering a dark room: press the light switch and the room is filled with light. Press your love switch and fill yourself with love.

'Remember that the soiled garment you shrink from touching may have been yours yesterday, may be yours tomorrow. And if you turn from horror from it, when it is flung on your shoulders, it will cling more closely to you.'

Mabel Collins, *Light on the Path*

RULE
YOUR
STATE

EXERCISE: MY BELIEFS ABOUT MY NEW WORLD

Uncover any limiting or disempowering beliefs by asking yourself the following questions. You can write your answers in your journal or in the back of this book and revisit them as you move along your path.

- ☀ What is changing in my world as a whole because of my wish manifesting in my life?
- ☀ Am I happy to be seen as successful?
- ☀ Am I happy to longer get sympathy for being a victim?
- ☀ Am I happy to no longer blame others for my life?
- ☀ Am I happy to attract new people into my life who have a positive mindset?

'They went to sea in a sieve, they did; In a sieve they went to sea; In spite of all their friends could say.'
Edward Lear, *The Jumblies*

EXERCISE: THE POWERFUL PAUSE

If you encounter emotional hijacking at any time, remove yourself as quickly as possible from the situation. If that is not possible, use the 'powerful pause' technique immediately. Here's how it works:

❀ First, change your emotional state by breathing deeply. Practising deep-breathing exercises will calm the mind.

❀ Next, label the emotions you are experiencing. Say out loud the name of the specific emotions. This interrupts your emotional state and has a calming effect.

❀ Finally, get your thinking brain back into play by asking yourself, 'What would I like to do now?' or, 'How can I see this situation differently?'

❀ Later, reflect on the emotions: what can you learn from what happened? What beliefs and values underlie these emotions when they appear in this context?

Long term, practising mindfulness or any kind of meditation practice will help you to better control your emotional state. It will also help you to have great communication between your conscious, subconscious and higher selves.

'What you see and what you hear depends a great deal on where you are standing. It also depends on what sort of person you are.'
C. S. Lewis

EXERCISE: JOURNAL AND CHALLENGE YOUR THOUGHTS

You can identify and challenge unhelpful thought patterns at any time. This exercise borrows from cognitive behavioural therapy (CBT), which helps you notice, question and replace negative beliefs with more empowering ones.

How to challenge a thought:

※ Notice: Pay attention to when you're experiencing a negative emotion and identify the thought linked to it. Ask yourself: what is the belief behind this feeling? Example: 'Speaking in public is scary.' (Emotion: Fear.)

※ Question: Ask yourself: what thought would I like to hold instead? What perspective might be more helpful in this situation?

※ Reframe: Write down a new, more constructive thought. Example: 'Speaking in public has scared me in the past, but with practice, I'll improve and maybe even enjoy it. Eventually, I could grow to love it.'

※ Test it: Try to prove your new belief by taking action. Prepare thoroughly for your next public speaking opportunity, or practise with a small group. Small wins will help reinforce your new belief.

※ Reflect: If the new thought doesn't quite feel right, adjust it until you find one that you believe and that helps you feel more capable. It should be both realistic and encouraging.

※ Repeat: The more you practise choosing and reinforcing helpful thoughts, the more flexible and adaptive your thinking becomes – and the more likely you are to create positive outcomes in your life.

When a past pattern reveals itself to you, it's an opportunity to learn new ways to deal with it. Journalling will help you learn from the experience and shift your perspective so you can think differently about it. The more you do this, the more you will find that you are able to self-regulate and choose your emotional reactions to situations.

EXERCISE: CHANGE EMOTIONS USING YOUR ARCHETYPES

You can learn to change your emotional state quickly and prevent negative emotions from controlling you by tapping into your archetypes.

※ When you're feeling negative, connect with your different archetype parts. Imagine them sitting in a circle around you. Ask what each of them thinks about the situation and hear their replies. Let them tell you how they would find a solution that takes you towards the result you want.

※ You can also imagine what it is like to feel the emotion you want to experience instead. Imagine you are connecting with the archetype who has the right energy to help you change your beliefs. Visualise yourself drawing on the energy of that part. As you access the part, you will notice your emotions changing. The more you 'fill out' your archetypes to give them power and character, the quicker you will be able to access them and the more helpful they will be. Remember, the quickest way to access them is use all your senses: visualise them, hear them, feel them in your body. Make the sound out loud, or say the words associated with your archetype. You can even imagine smelling their perfume or holding their hand.

※ When you enter a similar situation in the future, fire off the energy of the archetype who will get you out of the situation and provoke different behaviours.

'We have not even to risk the adventure alone, for the heroes of all time have gone before us. The labyrinth is thoroughly known ... we have only to follow the thread of the hero path.'
Joseph Campbell

STORY: THE BAKERY

Ginny had always had a crazy dream: to have a bakery. Her friends all scoffed at her. They told her she would never make any money from baking – after all, you could buy good cakes cheaply in any supermarket.

In her late twenties, Ginny went travelling around Europe. She took the train around France, Italy, Spain and Germany. She met many other travellers, and took one long train journey with a young man called Damien. She tasted lots of local cuisine and loved it. But when Ginny got home, she felt disappointed. She had seen firsthand how hard cooks and bakers and everyone in the hospitality industry worked. When she thought about the practicalities of getting up in the early hours of the morning to start baking, she wondered how much she really wanted it anyway. She was 28 years old.

Ginny decided that the bakery was indeed just a crazy idea, and instead she decided to go back to university to study geopolitics. She loved learning about different countries and how they interacted. By coincidence, she ended up working for a large international charity. A decade later, after spending some time in Africa, Ginny returned home and settled down.

One day, out of nowhere, the idea of the bakery

popped into her head again. What if she had been wrong? After all, she was competent at her job, she understood commerce and profit margins, and she had always been successful at maintaining good relationships with clients. Two days after she started thinking about her old dream, Ginny had a surprise contact through Facebook. It was Damien. He was now a food stylist working in advertising, and he'd clearly made a successful career of it. As she scrolled through Damien's social media pages, Ginny saw picture after picture of beautiful food, including some of the most delicious-looking doughnuts she'd ever seen. Damien reached out to say how nostalgic he was for the days when they had travelled around Europe. They met up for coffee, and it was as if no time had passed at all. They chatted for hours. Damien was sad to learn that Ginny had never pursued her dream career.

'It's never too late, you know,' he said.

Ginny went home that day with a new idea. It wasn't that she wanted to run a bakery: it was that she wanted to bake. She decided to take a course, and eventually got up the courage to post pictures of her cakes online. Within a year she had been contacted by a celebrity agent who commissioned one of her cakes, and within two years she had a thriving business. Ginny's dream had just needed a bit of a tweak.

THE APPROACH

'Consider nothing impossible, then treat possibilities as probabilities.'

David J. Schwartz

You can see a light in the distance along the path. You keep heading in the direction of the light. Sometimes the path goes dark, but the light is still there, even when it seems to have disappeared.

The approach is the part of the master story pattern that comes just before the reward. When you are waiting for a wish to come true, the universe needs you to keep faith. You must keep to the path and keep moving forward. Don't get lured off to the side. As you persist, your thinking evolves, your identity strengthens and you gain new skills and behaviours.

In *Star Wars*, this is the part of the story when Luke and his friends approach the Death Star. In *The Lion King*, it is when Simba gets ready to confront Scar. In *The Wizard of Oz* it is when Dorothy arrives in the Emerald City. In the ancient story of David and Goliath, it's the moment when David prepares to face the giant. On the approach, you must keep going. The world rewards those who never quit and who keep believing. Don't talk about what you want to manifest and the new life path you are taking; you will destroy the magic by diluting the potency of the path you are taking. Just take an action, then take another, and another. Slowly but surely, the actions you take will build the path between the wish you made and the fulfilment of that wish in the future.

'My advice is, never do tomorrow what you can do today. Procrastination is the thief of time.'

Charles Dickens
David Copperfield

HABITS MATTER

At this stage, habits matter. There would be no great stories if the main character just sat before the end of the path, waiting for the treasure to come to them. The universe helps you when you help yourself. Keep trusting the process – show up every day when no one is watching you, take consistent steps towards what you want, and you will magnetise your wish towards you. Remember, you never know when a seed you planted will pop its head up from the earth and become a flower. Every time you point yourself in the direction of your wish, you are doing something extraordinary. Sometimes you'll take a giant leap and be rewarded. At other times, you will manifest through a series of tiny steps. Just keep on the path and keep moving. Your future self will thank you.

It's true that a manifest is not a goal. Manifesting appears to play tricks on you. Sometimes you will have a wish come true easily. You visualise going to a concert, and then a friend texts and offers you a free ticket. Or you imagine having a wonderful summer with friends, and you're invited to join them on holiday. Each of us has some wishes which we find easy to visualise, and they just seem to turn up in our lives. It can happen in strange ways. Once I needed to book a flight, but I didn't have the money for the ticket. Then I broke some items in my home by accident, and when the insurance payout came through, it was exactly the amount of money I needed. There was another time, many years ago, when I needed some money. Out of the blue a friend asked to rent my spare room, suggesting exactly the amount I had programmed into the universe.

However, if you want to manifest something big, make sure you keep demonstrating intention, attention and expectation. Taking small actions aligned with what you want will keep reshaping your thoughts and pour energy into your new identity. Every step is a step along a new path towards your reward. In my imagination, I always see my personal journey towards my future life like the picture of the yellow brick road in the film of *The Wizard of Oz*. Dorothy keeps going along the path, even though she has no idea how she will get home.

'The road was one of those deceptive ones which crumple up into nothing at all when you put your best foot foremost.'
Constance Armfield, *Sylvia's Travels*

HOW TO BUILD YOUR NEW HABITS

The universe is always looking for proof of your intention, attention and expectation. Habits colour in your new world and new identity and tell the universe that you're serious. Small steps are great because when you repeat them enough, they become so automatic that you don't even have to think about them. For example, you don't have to spend much brain power deciding to brush your teeth because it has become a small, easy-to-remember step in your daily routine. That's what you want to achieve in constructing your new world.

For example, a step might be as simple as buying some new clothes that represent your new life, saving money and asking the universe to double it, or being abundant by donating to charity, confident that the universe will always bring you more of what you need. A physical activity can also be helpful. Sit down and write something – anything at all – if you want one day to be a novel writer. Walk around the neighbourhood and look at the houses you desire. Join new groups if you want to meet a new love. Intentionally clear out your closet to create room for your future partner's clothes.

New habits create new neural pathways in the brain. New habits create new thoughts and magnetise your wishes into reality. Your goal is to fully enter your new world, just like a character in a novel enters the new world. Old ways of thinking and doing are replaced deliberately by positive, affirming thoughts and habits. Think like an author. How would you write you into this stage of the story you are living?

EXPECTATIONS

Trust is our contract with an unknown future.

I was brought up to believe in contracts. I opened a bank account. I signed a contract with my employer. As soon as I put my signature on that contract, I assumed two things – that there would be a benefit for me and that the other party to the contract would hold to the contract no matter what.

Wishes are the same. A wish starts as a want, but when you create a future memory, it becomes a solid contract. Of course, you can still change your mind and dissolve the contract. I'm not a lawyer, but good contracts also have a cooling-off period. Sometimes you buy a new TV, get home, and regret your purchase immediately. Many institutions will give you a get-out clause and you have the option of cancelling the order or returning the product.

Manifesting is even better, because the universe

is much more generous that the average institution. It will cancel the order *any* time you want. There's a catch, though. The universe listens to what you consciously want, but also to your powerful subconscious mind. You may not *intend* to cancel the contract consciously, but the universe pays attention to your overall congruence.

DETACHMENT

You will often hear the word 'detachment' in relation to manifesting your wishes. This part can be confusing. How can you pay attention to what you want and remain detached? And why do you need to detach?

The universe helps those who pay attention without desperation. Trying to keep a 'death grip' around when and how your wishes materialise pushes them away. The implication is a lack of trust in the abundance of the universe and its role in the co-creation of what you want. Wanting isn't the same as believing. Detachment – a light attention – allows room for the wishes to come alive. You can't know the divine timing of your wish. If you cling too hard to the dates you have scripted into your future, revise them so you can put them to the back of your mind. By letting go of any urgency, we reduce unconscious resistance and fears that may block us from being successful. Over-attachment creates heavy vibrations, while detachment and trust magnetise positive results through lighter vibrational frequencies. Detachment is a sign of an abundant mindset. Attachment is a scarcity mindset.

Give space to your manifests to come in their own way. Sometimes when I 'post' a wish to the universe, I think of the ideal timing, and then I add a codicil. For example, I might say, 'I ask that this be realised in a way aligned with the highest good of all concerned,' and then I say, 'I ask that this be realised in a surprising way.' This way, I have no chance of second guessing the universe and won't be sitting there waiting for the wish to be delivered. I must surrender to the infinite wisdom and timing of my co-creator.

'The moment you doubt whether you can fly, you cease forever to be able to do it.'
J. M. Barrie, *Peter Pan*

THE SCIENCE BEHIND MANIFESTATION: The Pygmalion Effect

My Fair Lady, starring Audrey Hepburn, is a film classic. Our heroine, Eliza Doolittle, is moulded into the perfect society lady despite the fact she is a London-born, working-class Cockney. The story is inspired by the Greek myth of Pygmalion, a sculptor who falls in love with a statue he has created and makes her come alive so he can marry her. In the film, the professor who educates Eliza is clearly in love with his creation.

The 'Pygmalion effect' is the idea that if an authority figure or someone we respect has high expectations of us, we will perform better than if they have low expectations. Positive expectations are contagious. The positive expectations of someone we look up to influence our beliefs, and their perception of us influences the way we view ourselves. This then influences the actions we take, which in turn reinforces the beliefs that others hold about us. High expectations get us positive results; low expectations lead to worse outcomes. If you have internalised the negative labels that other people have given you, these will also influence your outcomes. Your receptiveness to good outcomes will shape your reality, especially when you are tested.

The Pygmalion effect will play a significant role in your

manifesting success. Some people are very internal in their decision making and don't take the advice of others. These people are much less influenced by the people around them. If you are an external thinker who likes to discuss your decisions with others, please be particularly cautious about sharing all of your wishes. As a rule of thumb, it is best not to share your heart's desire with anyone. The more your dreams are discussed, the more likely they are to get diluted. Even if your friends aren't openly trying to dissuade you from taking a big step forward, you may unconsciously pick up that their expectations of you are not as positive as your own. They are likely to be guided by how you've behaved in the past and not realise that you're in the process of significant and permanent change. What's more, some of your older friends or members of your family may not want you to change. They may like you exactly as you are in the current roles you fulfil in their lives.

'THE LITTLE RED HEN'

'The Little Red Hen' is an American folktale about the importance of doing things even when other people won't help you. It was first included in a collection in 1874 by Mary Mapes Dodge. The little red hen lives on a farm. One day she finds some corn. She asks the other animals to help her plant it, but no one does. When the corn grows, she asks for help to cut it, but no one wants to help. She asks for help to carry the corn to the mill, then to grind the corn, and finally to make bread. At no stage is anyone willing to help, so the little red hen does all the work herself. Of course, at the end, all the other animals want to eat the bread she has made, but it's too late. She did everything by herself, and the bread is her just reward.

THE SCIENCE BEHIND MANIFESTATION: The Habit Loop

Remember, that positive feeling is what keeps the brain motivated. If your subconscious enjoys doing something, it's going to want to encourage more of the same. Make sure you make your new actions and habits rewarding and easy to do. If a large action is daunting, just make it smaller – as small as possible so it feels like no effort at all. When you take rewarding actions, you create dopamine. The brain wants more of the same reward again, so pulls you towards taking similar actions. This habit loop is known as cue, routine and reward.

- ※ Cue: Create a trigger, e.g. play music associated with an archetype. This is the cue that initiates the new habit.

- ※ Routine: This is the actual behaviour or action that follows. In this case it may be mental – thinking about your archetype – or physical – taking action in the manner of your archetype or making the sound of your archetype for a greater connection.

- ※ Reward: Reward is the positive reinforcement that comes from habit. In this case it will be the satisfaction of observing how much more flexible you are in your thinking and behaviour from accessing different parts of yourself.

THE FINAL TRIAL

The innermost cave and the ordeal are pivotal points in the story where significant challenges come to the fore. This is the juncture where the main character must confront their greatest fears and inner conflicts. If you've wished for a big thing to happen in your life, you may get one final test from the universe. Here's how it works. Right now, you're excited. Some small things you want have begun manifesting. It looks as if the big thing you want is getting ready to appear in your life. And then, bang: a final test gets in the way. It looks like game over – but is it?

I know this has happened to me. I create a clear picture in my head of what I want. I feel the end result, I take action in the real world, but I'm blocked. I have a decision to make: should I carry on or not? If I carry on, I'm going to have to look deeply at why I'm manifesting these blocks. Do I really trust the universe to deliver?

The block always lies with your sense of who you are – your ego and all the beliefs that make up this identity. In the ordeal and the innermost cave, when you expose yourself to your new life, you are given this final chance to turn back to the past. The main character can turn off the path and everything they do will have been for nothing – or he can decide to address his inner conflict and truly transform who he is. Then his reward awaits in the external and internal worlds.

The ordeal is the decision point. The main character faces a 'belly of the whale' moment in which they will either succeed or fail. This is a crucial stage in the journey where the main character, having accepted the challenge, enters a period of intense struggle – often feeling consumed by forces greater than themselves. It is a time of deep introspection and transformation, where resilience and courage are put to the test. Here, the 'old self' begins to fall away, making space for the emergence of a stronger, renewed self.

In *Star Wars*, Luke Skywalker must go into the Death Star – a dark and dangerous place – to rescue Princess Leia. There he faces numerous dangers. What's more, Obi-Wan Kenobi, his mentor, sacrifices himself in a duel with Darth Vader to allow Luke to escape. These moments are huge tests of his courage and resolve. Finally, he takes part in the 'trench run' through the Death Star when he must fully learn to trust in the force so he can destroy the Death Star.

People get confused just before the reward. They think. 'Things are the same as they've ever been. I knew the old me was the real me. I wished for a new identity but it's impossible. The real me will always be exposed.' The mistake here is there is no 'real you'. Instead, there

are infinite versions of you that are possible at any juncture.

What you think of as the 'real you' right now is just one identity. Future you is your choice. Old patterns feel familiar and safe. That's why, in the master story pattern, the main character is challenged again and again along the path. He is asked, are you sure you want this new version of you more than the old version? He answers *yes*, and steps forward to receive his reward.

'We are all connected, like drops of water in an infinite ocean. What affects one, affects us all.'
Charles Kingsley, *The Water Babies*

THE SWORD IN THE STONE

The Sword in the Stone by T. H. White was one of my favourite stories growing up. It was written in the 1930s and perfectly illustrates the master story pattern and the progression from not understanding our power to fully realising it.

Set in medieval England, *The Sword in the Stone* is the story of a young orphan boy known only as Wart. One day, Wart gets lost in the Forest Sauvage while chasing a hawk. He encounters Merlyn, a wizard who becomes his mentor. Through Merlyn, Wart learns how to transform himself into different creatures. He becomes a fish, a hawk, an ant and a goose. Then he meets Robin Hood. Wart is then made squire to Kay, who is the son of his guardian.

Every encounter teaches Wart something new, but despite his magical powers, he has no status in the world. It is Kay who will be knighted and participate in a tournament. As the tournament approaches, Kay realises he has forgotten his sword. The only sword Wart can find is one stuck in a stone, which he pulls out. Of course, as we know from Arthurian legends, this is the sword which will decide England's rightful king. Wart's real name is Arthur, and he is in fact the son of Uther Pendragon, the former king. Wart is the heir to the throne, and he is crowned King of England.

MAGNETISE
YOUR
FUTURE

EXERCISE: ACTION AFTER ACTION

Every action you take sends a message to your subconscious – and to the universe – that you're serious about what you want. It creates momentum and attracts opportunities. Actions align your external world with your intentions and show how committed you are to your future.

1. Think of a small first step that assumes that your wishes will come true – then take it. For example, if you're hoping for a promotion or a new relationship, why not clear out old clothes that feel tied to a past version of yourself and treat yourself to something new.

2. Keep pointing your daily actions towards your manifesting goals. A good habit is one that can be sustained even on days when you are low in motivation. A good habit will lift your mood because it reminds you that everything is coming to you.

3. Rituals are very effective. Develop a regular routine such as lighting a candle and meditating or practising gratitude for five minutes in the evening. Daydreaming is a great ritual. Incorporate light vibrations into your daily routine by cleaning your space. Once a month, get rid of anything from your home that you instinctively feel is no longer 'you'.

4. Keep two manifesting lists – one for things you have manifested, one for things you still want to manifest.

5. Ramp up your appreciation. Think of a few small, random things you'd like to experience in the next few days, then let them go and see what the universe brings you. These rituals will reinforce your faith in synchronicities. For example, visualise a good friend calling you, imagine receiving an invitation to do something fun, or picture a stroke of good luck that reminds you just how fortunate you are. Then see what the universe brings your way.

6. Keep a 'future success' diary. In the diary, imagine your wishes have come true. Revisit this journal regularly, adding in extra detail about how the last week of approaching the reward contributed to your success. Write down all the clues that the path from your wishes inevitably led to successful manifesting. This creates an abundant and positive mindset.

7. Update your vision board with more colour and detail. Keep journalling.

'The best thing for being sad is to learn something. That is the only thing that never fails. You may grow old and trembling in your anatomies, you may lie awake at night listening to the disorder of your veins, you may miss your only love, you may see the world about you devastated by evil lunatics, or know your honour trampled in the sewers of baser minds. There is only one thing for it then – to learn.'

T. H. White, *The Once and Future King*

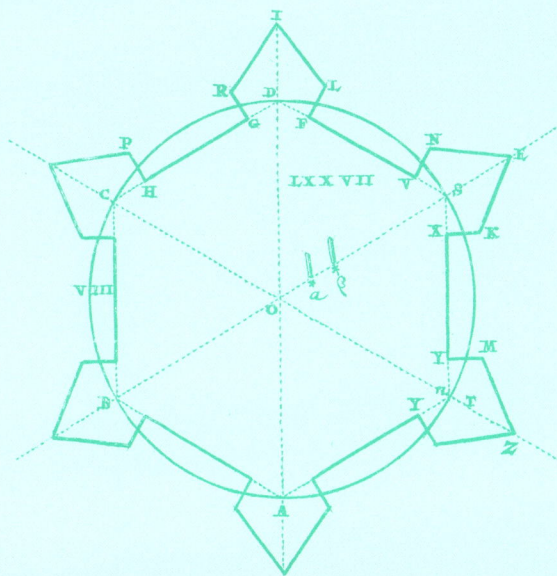

MY STORY: BEING RECEPTIVE

My father's mother was born in Norway, though she spent much of her life in Russia, Africa and India before settling permanently in the UK – so I never had the chance to visit. I often noticed how much I looked like her and began to wonder if I might fall in love with Norway, whether it would feel like home. It felt like somewhere I was meant to go, so I added it to my bucket list.

I found a picture of a Norwegian fjord and pinned it up on a vision board. I assumed that I would eventually arrange a trip with a friend, but with each year that passed, other things seemed to take priority. I often looked at the picture and wondered when I would ever get round to it.

Then one day, I finally decided it was time to find out more about my family's history in Norway. After some research, I came across two notable figures: one was a Norwegian politician in the nineteenth century, and one was a woman who was a writer. It was the second who caught my attention. I wanted to know more about her. But there was a problem – I don't speak Norwegian or Danish, and all the records were in those languages. With more searching, I uncovered a lovely professor who had written about her and who spoke English. Then the universe rewarded me further – she was coming to London with her husband. We met for lunch and she told me all about this amazing ancestor of mine, who was, in fact, the mother-in-law of the famous writer, Henrik Ibsen.

But what about my trip? Well, the universe had noticed I had an intention and had now paid some attention, and there were certainly no blocks to me being receptive to a trip to Norway. A couple of years later, out of the blue, I received an email from the professor. She had met a couple who lived in the house where my ancestor originally lived and had told them about me. She said this couple would love me to fly over and stay with them to celebrate the 200th anniversary of the writer's birth.

Of course, I took up the invitation. I ended up staying in a house with a garden backing directly onto the fjord, learning all about my Scandinavian heritage. It wasn't the way I expected the universe to deliver, but it shows that when you plant a seed, you can't control how it will bloom in your life.

STEP SEVEN:

THE REWARD

'Sometimes, I've believed as many as six impossible things before breakfast.'

Lewis Carroll,
Alice's Adventures in Wonderland

This final part of the master story pattern is the easiest part of the path. The light at the end of the path is nearer now, only a few steps away. The path still goes dark from time to time, but you can feel the light guiding you along it. If you look back from the present to the past, you can see the past still there, but you are a long way past the difficult peaks you had to climb and the dark swamps you had to navigate. It's all smooth sailing now. It's time to press on...

The final stage of the master story pattern is known as the stage of reward and resurrection. The reward is when your wishes finally manifest in the external world. The resurrection comes because, during the journey, you have undergone a process of growth and empowerment. You begin every journey with hope, but no knowledge of what is to come. You gain understanding of yourself as you move through the world you imagined. You fully embrace your new identity and see the splendour of the new world you have created with your wishes. Then, finally, you can end your journey and return home.

You have passed through trials and emerged from the depths of the ordeal. You have learned how to integrate your new self and your old one. This happens so subtly, and you've grown so accustomed to who you once were, that it may not be immediately clear to you that you are transforming – though it may be evident to others. You are taking the good bits from the old you and becoming one with the new you. It may even be that the parts of you that you mistook for weaknesses or loved least are the parts that you now love most. Notice how you respond to different people now, compared to how you used to respond. Pay attention to how consistently you now behave. Compare your new reactions to certain circumstances with your past reactions. Your external world has also changed in tandem with your internal world. Like a good detective, you can look in multiple places for clues that show just how immense the transformation has been.

As an example, in *The Wizard of Oz*, this is the stage where Dorothy has survived the ordeal of defeating the Wicked Witch of the West. She returns to the Emerald City, where she is given the promise of a way to return home to Kansas. The Scarecrow is promised a brain, the Tin Man a heart, and the Cowardly Lion, Courage. Then, in the resurrection, she is shown that the ruby slippers she has been wearing all along give her the power to return home by clicking her heels together three times. This discovery of her power is her inner treasure realised.

'And now here is my secret, a very simple secret. It is only with the heart that one can see rightly: what is essential is invisible to the eye.'
Antoine de Saint-Exupéry, *The Little Prince*

ALCHEMY

Often you will experience synchronicities or good luck which foreshadows your manifesting wish about to become reality. Then, your wish suddenly comes true. It's a wonderful moment, just as you envisioned when you transformed your wish into a future memory. Because you used your senses to encode your manifesting picture into your future, when it occurs, you feel that emotion again in your body as your future memory becomes a present reality. This is the moment of alchemy the mentor promised you.

ACKNOWLEDGE YOUR TRANSFORMATION

What did you wish for? A car, a home, new friends, a job, a relationship, a large cheque, your heart's desire? Take a moment to acknowledge what an amazing thing you have achieved. You received this reward because you stuck to the path, even when you were tested on your

willingness to renew your world. You have internalised whatever you needed to learn throughout your journey to enable the universe to reward you.

Let's pay tribute to your achievements. You have undergone a personal transformation. If you stop and look back at where you started your new story, you will see that you have shed the old you and embraced a new identity, overcoming old and limiting beliefs and fears. This is what has enabled the reward to come into your possession. Each reward you manifest, however or large or small, teaches you a new perspective on life. They prove to you that you are capable of breaking free of self-imposed limitations, overcoming challenges and manifesting your desired outcome.

MINDFULNESS

Mindfulness can be very helpful as a space for reflection when you have manifested successfully. Sitting quietly and reflecting on the journey you have taken can lead to profound personal understanding. You can use any insight you gain for the next journey you choose to take.

One important result of following this method is a greater ability to tune into your inner guidance and 'gut instinct'. You now have all the wisdom you need to guide you along any authentic path you choose to take next.

You have raised your vibration and opened your mind. Whatever your next wish and story, you will embark on it with new wisdom and self-understanding, fewer limits and a greater ability to mould your external world so it aligns with your authentic desires.

Because we are all connected, just by existing in this universe you impact everything around you. You are now raising the vibration and the consciousness of the world.

THE RETURN

This is what happens next. In stories, the main character goes back to where they started with their reward. Being mindful of what they have gained in each journey allows them to integrate their learnings and insights into their future life.

When you return home, even if your external rewards are not visible to others, your internal changes can't be hidden. The greatest reward that comes from a significant life change is a feeling of mastery and freedom. Once you have gone past your greatest fears, you are never at the mercy of lesser fears again. The main character who returns from a great adventure is not afraid of death, and so is no longer afraid to live and love. They understand their relationship with the

universe and truly recognise that all the power they will ever have is within them. They have destroyed illusions and self-delusion.

I love two moments in the *Wizard of Oz*. The first is when Dorothy finds out that the wizard is a fake and simply a showman, and the second is when she clicks her heels and discovers she could always go home. In *Alice's Adventures in Wonderland*, Alice goes down the rabbit hole and enters a world where nothing is as it seems. Alice's ultimate adversary there is the Queen of Hearts. She stands up to the Queen of Hearts during the trial of the Knave of Hearts, calling out, 'You're nothing but a pack of cards.' She then wakes up back in the real world. She has seen through the illusion of Wonderland, and she returns to tell her sister the stories she has acquired.

I wonder what stories you will have to tell – about your journey, your wishes, your adventures and the manifestation of your wishes into the real world.

WHAT'S NEXT?

What will you wish for next? One wish opens the door to another wish, and another, and another. One story winds into another, and there are always new decisions and choices to be made. Films have sequels for a reason. I'd love to hear about your sequel.

By manifesting all the wonderful things that you wished for in your life, you discover what matters and what doesn't matter. You now have the chance to stop and reevaluate, recalibrating the next set of wishes and making them truly meaningful. It's inevitable that what you think is the most important wish to manifest before you begin the story is not what you think is most important once you have trodden the path. Moreover, the more obstacles you encounter, the more you learn about yourself along the way. By embracing every aspect of the gap between the wish and its manifestation, you shift your mindset, removing the shackles of your previously limited way of thinking about what's possible for you. You may now find a deep new sense of purpose or calling.

You have an opportunity to examine whether your wishes have produced a balanced, desirable life, or whether you need to adjust and realign your next set of wishes with your life purpose. Have the wishes you manifested made a material difference to your life, or do you wish you had dreamed bigger? No problem – you can simply make a bigger wish now. Or perhaps you would rather carpet the next path with smaller wishes that will fill your life with enjoyment. Ideally, each set of wishes you create will be more and more aligned with your true self. The new challenges that you encounter in the external world will give you clues to any internal world conflicts that you are yet to resolve. In this case, create wishes that will expand your vision.

'If we want to solve a problem that we have never solved before, we must leave the door to the unknown ajar.'
Richard P. Feynman

THE POWER OF GRATITUDE

I invite you now to continue to practise gratitude for everything the universe has given you. You can also practise gratitude in advance for anything that you still wish to be given by the universe. This will maintain the loving and trusting relationship you now have with the universe. You will continue to move from scarcity to abundance in your thinking.

Gratitude practices are well-supported by science. When we are born, especially within the first five years, our brains are highly plastic. This means that our brains can develop connections incredibly quickly, and deep beliefs and habits can be ingrained, which sometimes last for the rest of our lives. These include deeply held ways of thinking about confidence, stress and safety. Unfortunately, if you have had trauma or stress in your life before the age of seven, your brain sets you up to be anxious, stressed and fearful later in life as well. Luckily, the brain can be rewired. Through practices like gratitude, mindfulness and learning new skills, you can create and strengthen new neural pathways. This will refocus your brain and reshape your emotions. Over time, the neural circuits associated with emotional regulation will be activated, and you will build long-term well-being. Positive thinking helps to reduce levels of cortisol in the body and instead stimulates the production of dopamine and serotonin, the neurotransmitters which regulate positive mood and behaviour. You will become more receptive to positive results, and your vibration will be raised as well.

As part of your journalling, practise gratitude: start or end your day by reflecting on the things you have in your life or things you experienced that day that you are grateful for. If you don't want to write them down, simply go over them in your mind's eye. I've been doing this ritual as I fall asleep since I was a child, saying thank you for three things, even in challenging times. There's always something to be grateful for.

STEP SEVEN
RESOURCES:

MANIFESTATION
MASTERY

EXERCISE: CHECK IN WITH YOUR ARCHETYPES

It's time to check in with your gang of friends – your archetypes. Over the course of your journey, you've got to know all of them. Some you will have a greater connection with than others. Look at the description you wrote down for each one. Hold each one in your imagination and notice again where they connect in your body. How does where they connect in your body reveal their qualities to you? If you have been accessing them regularly, you will be able to do this in seconds.

Think back to the journey you have taken. Which parts of you were most dominant? Now think to the future. Which parts of you would you like to access more of on your next journey? The ruler? The hero? The caretaker? Perhaps accessing the creator would help you to create bigger wishes next time? Perhaps the rebel would help you to create even more authentic wishes next time?

Listen to what they're telling you. Perhaps the hero is saying, 'come on, let's have another adventure!' Perhaps the creator is saying, 'This is exciting, my imagination is boundless.' Perhaps the ruler is telling you that you can manifest more physical possessions. Imagine them sitting down and coming up with their proposals for your future. Write them down, and use the

calm, sage part of yourself to adjudicate on the path you will follow next.

EXERCISE: DREAM ABOUT WHAT YOU WANT NEXT

Repeat the exercise from Step Two to manifest your new wishes using all your senses. Create a fresh and compelling picture of your new wishes using your senses and feeling what you will feel when your wish is fulfilled. Say thank you in advance and then let go.

TAKE AN ACTION FOR YOUR FUTURE

Every day from today, you can make a conscious decision to take an action which moves away from past identities, past habits and past beliefs, and towards the next world you want to script. Intentionally begin each day with the knowledge that you are pointing your actions towards your desired future and the version of yourself you aspire to be. This way, you are in always in a state of becoming or having reached your destination. If you catch yourself talking to people in a way that reflects an old version of you, correct your behaviour and align it with the version of yourself you aspire to be.

CONTINUE TO MANAGE YOUR EMOTIONAL STATE

As you have worked through this book, you will have learned

more about yourself and your emotions. The rewards you manifest on an external level will have given you a clue as to how successfully you have developed internally.

Everything you have done is a step – or several steps – towards emotional mastery. Abraham Hicks developed a scale of emotions called the emotional guidance system. At the top of the scale sit the emotions which raise your vibration most: joy, appreciation, empowerment, freedom, love. At the bottom are the lowest vibration: fear, grief, depression, despair, powerlessness. High-vibration emotions attract desirable experiences, while lower-vibration emotions may lead to unwanted manifests.

As you move through life, your ongoing mission is to eliminate or diminish the lower-vibration emotions in your life and maximise your high-vibration emotions. It only takes a second to get yourself into a better emotional state. You'll know you have complete emotional mastery when you can consciously shift any negative emotions to positive ones and sustain this positive emotional state so it becomes a lifelong habit. This can only attract better and better circumstances, people and synchronicities into your life.

ALPHA STATE WORK

As you continue on your next life journey, practising any form of quiet stillness – whether it's meditation, breathwork or

simply intentional calm – can help raise your vibration and give you greater consistency and control over your emotional state. Spending time in what's known as the 'alpha state' – a relaxed, wakeful state reached through these practices – is a powerful way to connect with your subconscious mind. In this state, we are calm, present and focused, without feeling tense or stressed. You can revisit any emotions that are blocking you, get in touch with what is really important in the next stage of your life, and speed up your wishes being fulfilled.

Movement, dancing, and exercising can also raise your vibration. I find that ideas flow better for me when I'm walking in nature or listening to a piece of music. It cuts out all the conscious noise. Choose high-vibration music which lifts your mood and makes you feel happy.

'The future is something which everyone reaches at the rate of sixty minutes an hour, whatever he does, whoever he is.'

C. S. Lewis

EXERCISE: JOURNAL AND REFLECT

You can keep using your journal in two ways.

1. Maintaining intention, attention and expectation: Regular journalling helps you to refine your thinking about the unlimited possibilities open to you. It encourages you to keep dreaming without critiquing your dreams, so you keep visualising your desired outcome. Practise this technique regularly, especially upon waking and before sleeping. This will help you to get better and better at visualising your wishes coming true.

2. Self-development: Keeping a journal to track your thoughts also allows you to identify triggers for unwanted emotions and eliminate them. Writing down your thoughts can also be a very mindful process if you sit quietly and spend some time on it. Use the journal prompts in the last section. You can also simply get a notebook and write freely in the morning or evening without critiquing what you write as another way of understanding yourself.

'Magic is always pushing and drawing and making things out of nothing.'
Frances Hodgson Burnett, *The Secret Garden*

STORY: THE FRUIT TREE

Far, far away it was said, there grew a magnificent, tall fruit tree. The stories said that its branches were wide and reached up to the sky, forming a beautiful natural cathedral laden with the most delicious fruit that had ever been tasted in the world. Its roots grew deep, deep into rich red earth.

Everyone in the land knew about the tree, and everyone desired once in their lifetime to taste its fruit. Each generation told tales of the tree and the journeys that had been taken to reach it, but the strange thing was that the journey was never the same.

One sailor found the tree on a beautiful island when he was 80. He had sailed from island to island in desperate desire and was about to give up hope when he found the tree nestled between two great rocks. It took him a day to climb up and reach the fruit.

A farmer rode his horse through grassland and forests in search of the tree. He fought off wild boar and giant eagles, and finally found it at the edge of a lake. He swam for 10 hours before he reached the tree.

A poet swore that he found himself beneath the tree after a day spent daydreaming in a field full of cows and tall grasses.

A young girl declared that she was taken to the tree at night in her dreams, flying on a magical dragon. There she tasted the fruit, and it was the most delicious thing in the world.

Each adventurer who found the tree and tasted the fruit made a map of their journey, but when a new traveller tried to follow another traveller's map, it took them to a different place. And yet when a traveller did find the tree, however long it took, they all said the same thing: it was as if the tree was waiting just for them. They sat under its quiet branches and picked the fruit and ate it. They heard the rustle of the wind in the leaves and were overcome with a feeling of peace in their heart.

Yet another strange thing was that each traveller described the fruit in different ways. One insisted the fruit had the flavour of a peach. Another argued it looked like an apple but tasted like the sweetest strawberry. A third said, no, the fruit was like the purest honey. They all agreed on one thing: their greatest desire was to return and taste the fruit again.

But when they tried to draw a map, all but the beginning of the map vanished in front of their eyes.

YOUR
12-MONTH
JOURNAL

'A hero ventures forth from the world of common day into a region of supernatural wonder: fabulous forces are there encountered and a decisive victory is won.'

Joseph Campbell
The Hero with a Thousand Faces

I hope reading this book has sparked some exciting thoughts about your future. If you have taken the time to make a wish, or more than one, you have already crossed the threshold from your old life into the new and have begun a new adventure. Always remember there are no restrictions other than those you impose on yourself. Let your feelings guide your wishes so they truly represent the greatest and most authentic expression of your potential. With each new adventure, you will find opportunities to make your new world the one you want it to be. You will take actions that stack one on top of another to create unstoppable, positive change.

This last section is your space to start a journal – a place to practise and strengthen your manifesting habits. You might want to photocopy these pages or simply copy the prompts into your own notebook.

The prompts and exercises included in this section are designed to help you clarify your intentions and learn how to define what you truly desire. By reflecting regularly on your inner purpose and feelings, you can manifest at the deepest level the things that are important to you personally.

There is no strict rule about how often to write, but once you get into the habit, you might find it becomes something you look forward to every day. Let it inspire you to take small, meaningful actions daily. Over time, these manifesting habits will become second nature, helping you master the art of creating the life you want.

Every day brings new possibilities for happiness, excitement, joy and an authentic expression of the you that you choose to be. There will be smooth paths, and from time to time there will be boulders and obstacles along the road. These tests are always a chance for you to readjust, to learn and to appreciate the inner change that is taking place and that will guide your outer journey.

HOW TO USE YOUR JOURNAL

A good way to start is to journal consistently for 30 days. After that, revisit your wishes, refine them and keep tracking your progress over the year. Document your thoughts, feelings and wishes, celebrate your successful manifesting and express gratitude every time you manifest what you wished for.

As you journal over the coming weeks and months, you will find yourself changing. As your new story gains momentum and you see your wishes manifesting in your life, I encourage you to notice how you are also changing internally. The more you allow yourself to dream, and the more you inspire yourself to manifest really satisfying change in your life, the less you will engage with any negative self-fulfilling prophecies. Finally, you will shift your beliefs at a deep level and cultivate an amazing positive mindset that aligns with what you want to manifest.

This is a personal journal just for you. Enjoy it. The path to your own greatness comes from within you. There is no one here to judge you for what you write. This is for your own self-exploration.

Treat this book like you would a notebook – scribble all over it, draw pictures, even scrapbook in it. I want you to make it your own. Each day, imagine what is possible. Stretch your imagination as far as it will go and dream. This is your chance to rewrite your story again and again.

And by the end of the year, if not well before that, you will have a new story to tell the world.

'Life isn't about finding yourself.
Life is about creating yourself.'
George Bernard Shaw

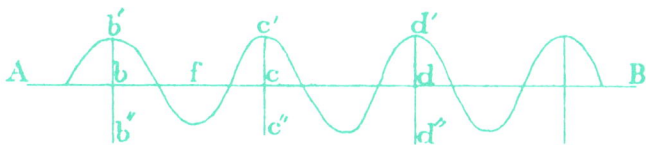

PROMISE YOURSELF

Begin by making a contract with the universe.

I am ready to make my wishes come true and make this my best year ever.

Sign your name here:

_____

'Live, travel, adventure,
bless, and don't be sorry.'
Jack Kerouac

MORNING JOURNAL

Use this page every morning. Start your day by tuning in to your thoughts and setting your intentions.

PAY ATTENTION: When you wake up in the morning, scribble down any thoughts you have about yourself and your manifesting goals. Notice any blocks and obstacles that have come to your attention. They are the stepping stones to your greatest growth.

CREATE INTENTION: Focus on what you want. Spend five minutes visualising your day ahead and what you would like to happen. Take a moment to imagine how you want to feel for the rest of the day.

HAVE AN EXPECTATION: Say thank you in advance for what you expect to happen today.

'For within you is the light of the world –
the only light that can be shone on the path.'
Mabel Collins

EVENING JOURNAL

Use this page every night. End your day with reflection, gratitude and focused intention for tomorrow.

PAY ATTENTION: Write down any thoughts you have about how your day went.

EXPRESS GRATITUDE: Write down what you are grateful for today.

_____

_____

_____

_____

_____

CREATE INTENTION: Focus for five minutes before bedtime on what you are seeking to manifest.

_____

_____

_____

_____

'Who in the world am I?
Ah that's the great puzzle.'
Lewis Carroll, Alice's Adventures in Wonderland

WEEKLY JOURNAL

Complete this exercise once a week. Pause to review your progress and plan your next steps.

Notice what happened during this week. Think about the people you have met and the experiences you have had in the external world, including any signs that you are on track to manifesting what you want. Notice any obstacles that the external world has brought to your attention as well as any internal world clues, such as unwanted thoughts. What will you do differently next week? What will you continue? Are there any exercises that you can revisit from the step-by-step chapters?

Write down where you think you are on your journey, between Step One and Step Seven:

_____

_____

What do you need to keep doing?

_____

_____

What do you need to stop doing?

_____

_____

What do you need to start doing?

_____

_____

'If I were writing a book I might make mistakes.
But God knows how to make the story end just
right – in the way that's best for us.'
E. Nesbit

MONTHLY JOURNAL

Complete this exercise once a month. Take time to dream big, clarify your vision and celebrate your growth.

You are the best author in the world. Each month you can re-edit your wishes and any aspect of yourself to make them materialise faster and with more accuracy.

Use this time to revisit all the big changes you would like to manifest. The magic happens when you write in the present tense, truly imagining that your wishes have come true. The more details and emotion you can include in your description of your future state or destination for your life, the more effective your scripting will be. Think again about why you want to change this aspect of your life. Be grateful that your life is changing every day.

Imagine your good health as the foundation of your life. Imagine the person you have become, the friends you have gained. Imagine your perfect relationship with loved ones. Script your material successes, your financial abundance, your great career, your life purpose and your spiritual meaning. Visualise and write about your adventures, your home, your daily environment and the impact you are having on the world around you, as well as any legacy you are leaving.

Make sure you include your heart's desire.

'Imagination has given us the steam engine,
the telephone, the talking machine, and the
automobile, for those things had to be dreamed of
before they became realities.'
L. Frank Baum

EXTRA MONTHLY EXERCISES

Try any of these exercises to deepen your
manifesting practice:

Write a letter from your future self to your present self. Tell
yourself about all the amazing changes you made in your life
and thank your past self for taking the journey. Congratulate
yourself for specific steps you took.

❀❀❀❀❀❀❀❀❀❀❀❀❀❀❀❀❀

List out the obstacles you have encountered. Recognise what
you can learn from them that will allow you to use them
as opportunities to accelerate your journey to what you
want to manifest.

❀❀❀❀❀❀❀❀❀❀❀❀❀❀❀❀❀

Pay attention to your dreams and any symbols and themes that
you observe. Often they give you clues to any thoughts, fears
and hopes you may have about your new life.

❀❀❀❀❀❀❀❀❀❀❀❀❀❀❀❀❀

Do a ritual to let go of past hurt. Write down anything that
has hurt you this month or the names of anyone you feel has
hurt you. Imagine you are forgiving them. Channel white light

through the top of your head towards the piece of paper. See yourself releasing the hurt from your body. End the ritual by burning the paper.

❀❀❀❀❀❀❀❀❀❀❀❀❀❀❀❀❀

Write down any limiting beliefs and the beliefs you would like to hold instead. Write down how you intend to reinforce these new beliefs and make them part of your new life.

❀❀❀❀❀❀❀❀❀❀❀❀❀❀❀❀❀

Deepen your connection with your archetypes. Make a note of how they appear to you. It's helpful to describe what they look and sound like. Where do they live in your body? Ask them about any dilemmas you have. Listen to what they tell you.

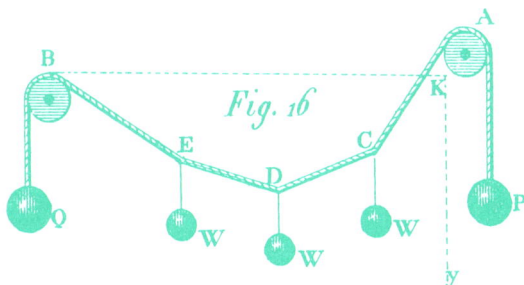

Fig. 16

'But then I realised, what do they really know? This is MY idea, I thought. No one knows it like I do. And it's ok if it's different, and weird, and maybe a little crazy.'
Kobi Yamada, *What Do You Do with an Idea?*

JOURNAL PAGES

JOURNAL PAGES

JOURNAL PAGES

JOURNAL PAGES

JOURNAL PAGES

JOURNAL PAGES

JOURNAL PAGES

JOURNAL PAGES

JOURNAL PAGES

JOURNAL PAGES

JOURNAL PAGES

JOURNAL PAGES

JOURNAL PAGES

JOURNAL PAGES

JOURNAL PAGES

JOURNAL PAGES

JOURNAL PAGES

JOURNAL PAGES

JOURNAL PAGES

JOURNAL PAGES

JOURNAL PAGES

JOURNAL PAGES

JOURNAL PAGES

JOURNAL PAGES

JOURNAL PAGES

JOURNAL PAGES

JOURNAL PAGES

JOURNAL PAGES

JOURNAL PAGES

JOURNAL PAGES

JOURNAL PAGES

JOURNAL PAGES